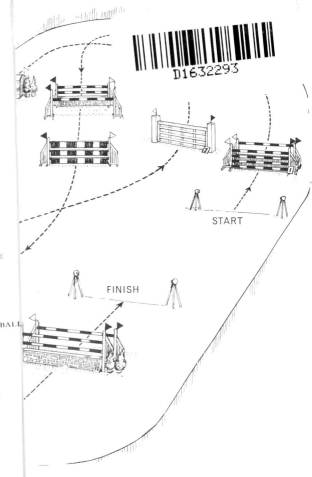

D1632293

START

FINISH

The Observer's Book of
SHOW JUMPING & EVENTING

VIVIEN BATCHELOR

WITH 44 LINE DRAWINGS BY
CHRISTINE BOUSFIELD AND
27 BLACK AND WHITE
PHOTOGRAPHS BY LESLIE LANE

FREDERICK WARNE & CO LTD
FREDERICK WARNE & CO INC
LONDON : NEW YORK

LIBRARY OF CONGRESS
CATALOG CARD NO 75–8055

ISBN 0 7232 1551 0

Printed and bound in Great Britain by
Morrison & Gibb Ltd, London and Edinburgh
548.875

CONTENTS

Acknowledgements

The artist would like to thank Mr Alan Ball and Mr Alan Hales for their kind advice in connection with the illustrations.

FOREWORD

As one who has spent a lifetime in the world of show jumping I have been impressed in recent years at the increased interest in the techniques of the sport shown by the ordinary members of the public. At one time they were content simply to see whether a horse cleared the obstacle or knocked it down. Now they are beginning to be interested in whether a horse and rider are approaching a fence correctly – one can often hear comments from the stands.

There is no doubt, then, that the man in the stands and the man sitting in front of his television screen is certainly taking a far deeper interest in the show jumping game than ever he did even ten years ago. So I am glad that the author of this book has taken on the task of increasing the ordinary man's enjoyment of the sport still more, by enabling him to follow the rules of the competitions in greater detail and to know what is required of horse and rider in each contest.

This volume should fill a long-felt want. It is easily carried in the coat pocket to a show, or placed on the arm of a chair. It gives, in simple language, a comprehensive guide not only to show jumping, but to Eventing and dressage – and the rules which govern each branch of the sport. It also gives the reader information on the history of the sport and the leading riders, and some of the most famous horses. Illustrations of typical fences both on cross-country and show jumping courses will help bring the sport to life for the follower on television, and aid the enthusiast who is attending the show or Horse Trials in deciding which fences are the most exciting to watch.

The author has been the equestrian correspondent of the London *Evening Standard* for many years and also wrote regularly in the *Horse and Hound* and other equestrian publications. Her book should provide the reader with a deeper knowledge, and therefore a greater enjoyment, of what is one of the fastest-growing spectator sports in the world.

<table>
<tr><td>Chairman B.S.J.A. Rules Committee</td><td rowspan="5">George Hobbs
Bucks Green,
Sussex. 1975</td></tr>
<tr><td>Royal International Horse Show Committee</td></tr>
<tr><td>International Affairs Committee</td></tr>
<tr><td>Horse of the Year Show Committee</td></tr>
<tr><td>Olympia and Cardiff Horse Show Committee</td></tr>
</table>

THE EARLY DAYS

Men with horses have been competing against each other for thousands of years, since the days of the Roman chariot races and before, but it was only in the last century that show jumping began to be thought of as a sport. Even then it was considered a rather bizarre off-shoot of equestrianism, not in any way likely to overshadow the serious business of horse shows which were mostly concerned with the display of hunters, hacks, and harness horses. Such jumping as there was in those days was mainly confined to the Continent and the crack cavalry regiments. That it was so slow to catch on in Britain is surprising when one considers our great hunting tradition and the prodigious jumping feats performed for centuries in the hunting field.

In the early days the term 'show jumping' was not used, the sport, such as it was, being termed simply 'horse leaping'. Then, as now, Ireland appears to have been one of the leading exponents of the art and records show that at the Dublin Show in 1865 there were classes for 'leaping'.

More than ten years later leaping classes were included in the programme of the great five-day agricultural show then held at the famous Agricultural Hall, Islington, in London. However, it was still considered such a novelty, and not to be taken very seriously, that no entry fee was charged for horses entered in the show classes if they wished to compete over the fences. The idea of horses specially trained for jumping still seemed very far-fetched.

But if we in Britain were slow to recognize the possibilities of the new sport, other countries were forging ahead. In America the first National Horse

Show in 1883 at Madison Square Garden, New York, included 'leaping' competitions, and by the end of the century show jumping had become firmly established as a sport in Germany and France. Competitions were still mainly confined to 'high jumps' and 'long jumps' and there appears to have been little real organization or compliance with any set rules. Soon the term 'leaping' was dropped and replaced by 'show jumping'.

By the turn of the century, show jumping had become an accepted sport on the Continent, and had begun to adopt an international flavour. At the World Fair in Paris in 1900 four countries were represented in the show jumping event, but Britain was not one of them.

However, in 1907, a great stride forward was made in this country. The first International Horse Show was staged in London at Olympia. Advertised as 'Open to the World', the show was the brainchild of the late R. G. Heaton, then managing director of Olympia, and the first president was the fifth Earl of Lonsdale, known as the 'Yellow Earl' as all his carriages and liveries were yellow. The earl was delighted to be asked to assume the office of president and he showed tremendous imagination and energy, continuing in the job for twenty-six years.

As it does today, the International Show of 1907 lasted a full week and the affair was a glittering social occasion with set rules of dress for the spectators: 'rat-catcher' for the morning sessions, silk hat and frock-coat or morning dress for the afternoons, and full evening dress for the evening. The catalogue for that first show weighed 1.13 kg ($2\frac{1}{2}$ lb)!

The international flavour was assured from the first by including men from America and Europe on the board and as judges. There were classes for officers' chargers, ridden hunters, and twelve jumping classes 'open to the world', including 'high' jumps and 'wide' (formerly known as 'long') jumps. The Belgians and the Dutch dominated the lists of prize winners in the jumping classes.

But in the early days the rules for judging remained haphazard and very much at the judges' discretion. Indeed it is reliably reported that during one of the early competitions for the Daily Mail Cup, then the major show jumping award, a rider fell off between two fences, but remounted and was given a clear round and declared the winner. Technically he had of course cleared the fences, but today the fall of horse or rider would incur 8 faults.

In the same year that the first International Show was held at Olympia (it was some years later before it received its present 'Royal' prefix), an international flavour was introduced across the Atlantic. The National Horse Show in New York invited riders from other countries to compete. Britain sent a team of Army officers, one of whom was the winner of a major competition.

For some years the superiority of foreigners over our own riders in show jumping was demonstrated annually at Olympia. The first team cup (a forerunner of the present Nations Cup competitions) was given in 1909 by H.M. King Edward VII, after whom it was named. It was won in that year by France who captured it again in 1911, Belgium taking it in 1910. For the next three years in succession the cup was won by the Russians entitling them to keep it, but after they took it back to Russia for the third time it was never seen again. Presumably it fell a victim either to the First World War or to the Revolution.

At the Olympic Games in 1908 an attempt was made for the first time to include equestrian events but this proved abortive; however, in 1912, when they were held in Stockholm, Count von Rosen of Sweden, the Olympic Games secretary-general, was very keen to have equestrianism included in the Games, and he persuaded the Olympic Committee to stage three events. These consisted of a Three-Day Event (in those days known as a 'military' since it was almost exclusively made up of cavalrymen); a dressage event; and show jumping. Then, as now, awards were given for both teams and individuals. The course was described as 'very difficult', although compared with today's standards it would not have seemed so. In those early days the training of both horses and riders had not been developed on anything like the scale or with the scientific knowledge which exists today. Maximum height of the fences was about 1.37 m (4 ft 6 in.), whereas in a modern Olympic course they are up to 1.70 m (5 ft 7 in.) or more. A water jump was included in that first Olympic course; it was 3.96 m (13 ft) wide. Today the rules stipulate that even for an Area International Trial (see p. 31) the water jump must be at least 4.27 m (14 ft) wide.

At those first equestrian Olympics France took the Gold Medal in the individual section. Germany was 2nd and Belgium 3rd. In the team competition the Gold Medal went to the host nation, Sweden, with France 2nd and Germany 3rd, followed by the U.S.A., Russia and Belgium.

Although the advent of the First World War virtually brought sport to a halt in Europe, across the Atlantic an important step was taken in the world of show jumping in 1917. Mr R. C. Vanderbilt, who had been the prime organizer of the New York National Horse Show, started the American Horse Shows Association, which is now the organizing and official body for the horse show circuit in the United States.

In the early 1920s came an event which was to

change the whole concept of equestrian sport (other than racing) throughout the world. It was the formation of the Fédération Equestre Internationale (F.E.I.) which today is the ultimate ruling body for international show jumping and Eventing and for dressage. Through the F.E.I. the rules for the Olympic Games equestrian events and for all major international shows are laid down. The present president is the Duke of Edinburgh whose interest is not only lively but practical, for he often offers outspoken though constructive criticism of international equestrian affairs.

At about the same time, on the home front, another association was formed which was to co-ordinate the sport nationally, and eventually bring British prestige and performance to the high standard, both of riders and horses, enjoyed today. This was the formation of the British Show Jumping Association. The early task of the association was to draw up a set of rules which would apply to all competitions. Up till then judging had been mainly a matter of individual interpretation by judges who were stationed one at each fence, and who alas were sometimes known to turn a blind eye! In those days marks were lost for touching a fence with hind legs or forelegs as well as for actually knocking it down, and the marks lost for knocking down varied as to whether the hind or forelegs had touched, and on spreads there were yet more varying penalties for the feet touching the lines of demarcation.

It will be seen, then, that the time had come to simplify the rules. Today the rules are universal for all shows affiliated to the British Show Jumping Association and vary only according to the type of competition. They can be readily followed by competitors, judges and the public, and this undoubtedly contributes towards the tremendous popularity of show jumping as a spectator sport either 'live' or on television. Those watching can keep their own scores and work out the results almost as soon as they are announced by the judges.

Between the two world wars, however, there was one element in which the British failed so disastrously that for a time public interest in show jumping seemed to fade away completely and it was dropped from the programme of a number of the bigger agricultural shows. That element was time. The British took years to catch up with riders from the Continent and America in jumping against the clock, for this had not been included in the original B.S.J.A. rules. The result was that, almost without exception, when we came to compete abroad our riders were beaten by the time limits. It was probably the succession of failures suffered by our riders when they went abroad that played a large part in the falling off of public interest in the sport.

Then came the Second World War – and this was to change the whole picture. In a prisoner-of-war camp in Germany, at Spannenberg, was a group of British cavalry officers who had been in British show jumping teams in the '30s and who had retained their enthusiasm and belief in the sport. They whiled away many incarcerated hours talking show jumping to their fellow prisoners, planning new types of fences and courses, discussing peacetime plans. Among them was Col. Mike Ansell (now Sir Mike Ansell), who in the last thirty years has done more for show jumping, not only in Britain but throughout the world, than any other single individual – and this in spite of being blinded in the war before being taken prisoner.

When they were eventually repatriated Col. Mike Ansell and his friends set about reviving the nearly defunct British Show Jumping Association, and Col. Ansell was elected chairman. With great courage they arranged a Victory Show Jumping

Championship in 1945 to be held at the White City with a first prize of £100 – the biggest sum ever offered at that time. The course was carefully designed and all the theories so often discussed in the prisoner-of-war camp were put into practice. The result was that for the first time in Britain jumps were made so that the horses could see them – brightly painted poles and fences – and distances were carefully measured to take into account the length of a horse's stride. Needless to say some riders deemed the course unjumpable and refused to enter, but others, such as Ted Williams, Wilf White, 'Curly' Beard and Phil Blackmore, whose names were to continue to hit the headlines in the sport for many years, decided to 'have a go' and not only they but the public were delighted. Among those who afterwards admitted sitting on the edge of their seats with excitement was Frank Gentle, the chairman of the Greyhound Racing Association, who owned the White City stadium.

The success of the 1945 show led to the rebirth of the International Horse Show in 1947, this time held not indoors at Olympia, but out of doors, in midsummer, at the White City stadium. It was to continue at the White City for nearly twenty years until rebuilding operations drove it to Wembley. In 1957 it became the Royal International Horse Show, and it is now one of the major shows of the world. A little later the Horse of the Year Show was to be inaugurated, originally at Harringay and later also moved to Wembley, an October fixture which marks the climax of the summer show jumping season and about which there will be more to say later.

At the same time as show jumping was catching the public imagination and Britain's prestige abroad and in the Olympics was soaring, another branch of equestrian sport was rapidly expanding. This was the Three-Day Horse Trial or Event, which had virtually been non-existent before the Second World War in the form in which we know it today. It started to develop from the time when the Duke of Beaufort watched the Three-Day Event held at Aldershot as part of the 1948 Olympic Games which were staged at Wembley. Sixteen nations competed of whom eleven were eliminated, including Great Britain. The duke was fascinated by the sport and determined to see Britain do better. He offered his beautiful parkland at Badminton in Gloucestershire as a course for the British Horse Society (which is to Eventing what the British Show Jumping Association is to show jumping) to stage what was then called 'Olympic Horse Trials'. The original idea was simply to train a team for the next (1952) Olympics so that they would compete with more finesse and distinction than had been managed in 1948.

In 1949, then, the first Trials, now known as the Badminton Horse Trials (and which have become among the most prestigious in the world), were staged. Although the weather was bad, more than 6,000 people turned up to watch this new-fangled 'sport'. Most of them were completely mystified by the dressage section, while the cross-country immediately caught on with the enthusiasm of a Grand National, and the show jumping phase was of course intelligible to all.

Other Trials followed. Harewood provided sport for the north and a second full Three-Day Event. The Harewood Trials were held in Yorkshire on the estate of the late Princess Mary, Countess of Harewood, who was a keen enthusiast of the sport. Eventually, however, changes in the agricultural policy of the estate made it impossible to allow use of the land, and the Harewood Trials became defunct.

Fortunately for the sport, however, Lord Burghley, himself an Olympic athlete, offered the use of his estate near Stamford, and so the Burghley Horse Trials became part of the late summer calendar. European and World Championships have been held there several times.

The Army had always held its own Trials at Tidworth, but gradually, with the growth of interest not only by spectators but by riders as well, more and more civilians entered until Tidworth became in effect a civilian event although special prizes are still given for Army riders. The Trials have been extended into a Three-Day Event, though the course is not considered so testing as that at Badminton or Burghley.

With the ever-growing popularity of Eventing many organizers began to introduce One- or Two-Day Trials. In these the horses still undertake Dressage, Show Jumping and Cross-country tests, but the scale and severity are cut down. They provide great opportunities for riders of good hunter-type horses to try their luck, and many graduate from these to the bigger Trials. Indeed, to be able to enter the big Events today horses must have completed a number of One- or Two-Day Trials.

These smaller Events provide an opportunity for spectators to watch the sport near their homes, for during the season there are Trials held in some part of the country every week and they provide a wonderful family outing for all who love horses and the open air.

THE SHOW JUMPING COURSE

The course, naturally, is a very important part of a show jumping competition, and today course building is a highly skilled, scientific art. The British Show Jumping Association has a panel of official course builders most of whom have graduated from being either competitors or judges. At all the major shows one of these builders is invited to design the course, but at many small shows the organizers may simply hire a set of fences and build their own course. One of the top course builders is a woman, Mrs Pam Carruthers, who is the course builder at Hickstead and who built the course for the 1974 World Championship. She is often invited to build courses in Canada and America. The other senior course builder is Alan Ball who is responsible for the indoor courses at Wembley as well as indoor and outdoor courses at dozens of other shows. From time to time the B.S.J.A. holds lectures and demonstrations on the art of course building so that show organizers may receive some expert advice, but at present there is no equivalent to the Instructors' examinations (for riding instruction) or Stable Management examinations in the course-building field.

As important as the obstacles themselves which, provided they comply with certain set rules, can give the builder scope for imagination, are the distances between them. These provide the real test, together with the grouping of the three basic types of fence: the straight or upright fence; the spread fence, where the horse must extend itself to achieve width as well as height in his jump (included in this category is the water jump); and a combination fence where two or more varying types of fence are placed so that they follow each other closely, the maximum distance between them not exceeding 12 m (39 ft 4 in.).

The straight fence may consist of a simple pole attached to two uprights, but this is in fact very difficult for a horse to assess. A horse judges its take-off from the line at the base of the obstacle. For this reason, several poles or planks one above the other, a wall or a gate give a horse a fairer task. According to B.S.J.A. rules the first obstacle in any competition must not exceed 1.22 m (4 ft) in height except in the case of a jump-off, and it must be solid and inviting to the horse, and therefore must not be a 'straight' fence. This last stipulation is to enable the horse to get his eye in and to obtain an easy, flowing rhythm.

There are a variety of spread fences, the most common being the triple bar – a series of three rails placed one behind the other in increasing heights, the first being usually not more than 0.61 m (2 ft). The height of the third and final rail varies according to the width of the spread (the distance between each set of rails), the higher the rail, the wider must be the spread. The B.S.J.A. rules are that no spread may exceed 2 m (6 ft 7 in.) in width with the exception of that used in a puissance competition, or in the case of water. The rules for water are that the face of the water must not be less than 4.27 m (14 ft) except in the case of an indoor course when it is reduced to 3.65 m (12 ft), or in the case of Junior or Grade C (novice) competitions when it must not exceed 3.65 m (12 ft) except in a jump-off. Usually a small brush fence is laid in front of the water to encourage the horse to take off.

Sometimes a course builder will place a ditch under or in front of, or behind, a fence. This then becomes a normal spread fence and is not classed as a water jump. In this case the face of the water must not be more than 1.83 m (6 ft).

Another type of spread fence is the 'oxer', which consists of a hedge, either movable or, in some permanent courses, growing, with rails on the take-off and landing side. Rules state that the two top rails on the take-off side and the top rail of the landing side must be visible so that the height and width of the fence cannot be mistaken. The tricky part of an oxer is that a horse judging its ground line as the base of the hedge does not always realize that the rail is often up to 0.61 m (2 ft) nearer to him. This of course is where the skill of the rider in guiding the horse comes in.

The 'hog's back', as its name suggests, is another triple spread, but with the middle rail placed higher than the first and third which are usually equal. A brush 'fill-in' is often put under the first pole to give the horse his ground line.

Parallel poles make one of the most difficult spread fences for a horse to tackle, as there is no ground line, and the fact that the poles are parallel makes it difficult to judge the width. In fact, in many competitions except those of the highest class, a 'filler' of some sort is used under the poles, or the first pole is fractionally lower than the others.

As has already been stated, a combination fence is really two or more obstacles placed to follow each other within a set distance not exceeding 12 m (39 ft 4 in.). The object of this type of obstacle is to test the skill of horse and rider in adjusting the horse's speed and stride, and this is what the rider must decide upon when he walks the course before the competition.

In theory a horse jumping over an obstacle describes a semi-circle and lands the same distance away from a fence as that from which he took off, and the distance between these points is equal to the

TRIPLE BAR

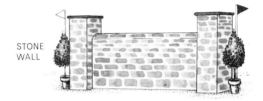

STONE
WALL

PLANKS

GATE

SHOW JUMPS - 1

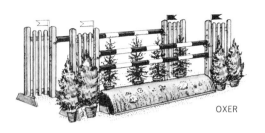

OXER

CROSSED POLES
(AACHEN)

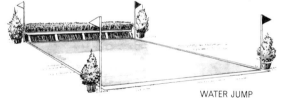

WATER JUMP

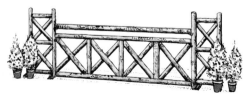

SHOW JUMPS-2

FANCY RUSTIC & RAIL

ROAD CLOSED

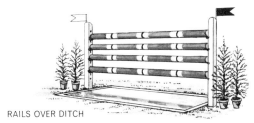

RAILS OVER DITCH

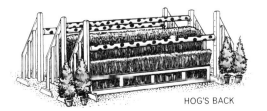

HOG'S BACK

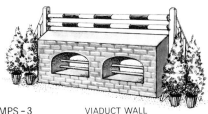

SHOW JUMPS - 3   VIADUCT WALL

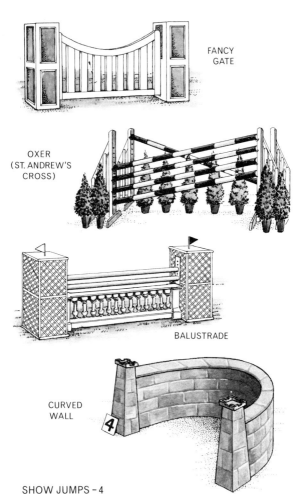

FANCY GATE

OXER
(ST. ANDREW'S
CROSS)

BALUSTRADE

CURVED
WALL

SHOW JUMPS – 4

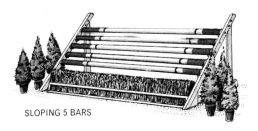

SLOPING 5 BARS

PALISADE

PLANK
OXER

HICKSTEAD
ROAD JUMP

SHOW JUMPS - 5

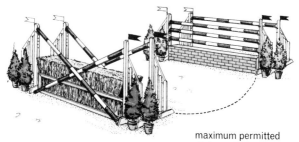

maximum permitted
distance between
elements: 12 m (40 ft)

TWO TYPICAL 'DOUBLES'

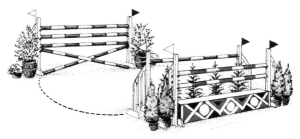

THE 'TREBLE':
A DIFFICULT COMBINATION

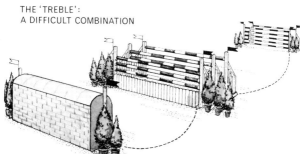

SHOW JUMPS – 6

height of the fence. This of course *is* only theory and the distance varies according to the horse's individual style. The faster the horse is travelling, the further out he will take off and land, and the higher the fence, the further out he will land.

The course builder, in setting up the combination, will have in mind that the average horse's stride at canter is about 3.66 m (4 yd). If, however, for some reason, such as a sharp turn in the course, he slows down, his stride may be reduced to 2.44 m (2 yd 2 ft).

The distance, then, between the elements of a combination (usually there are three, one of which is often a spread) is determined by the speed at which the horse can be expected to be travelling, and the type and height of fence for a particular element. If the second fence is higher than the first, the horse will land further out and so the distance between the second and third fence must be lengthened, but if the third element is a spread, then the distance may need to be reduced to enable the horse to make the width. And always the builder must work within the set distance, for if this is exceeded, the obstacle, instead of being part of a combination, becomes a separate fence. He must also avoid trick distances which might turn the combination into a dangerous trap.

When the rider walks the course he must decide how many strides the builder has allowed for, not only between all the fences but especially between those in the combination, and how best he can adjust this to his own horse's performance. It is on the skill and intelligence of these calculations that competitions are often lost or won. For instance, in the case of a treble combination, should he approach fast and land well over the first part, probably reaching the second in two strides; or should he make a slower approach and so have to fit in three strides; and if so, will this give him enough impulsion to clear the second and give him proper take-off for the third. And if that third element is a spread, will he be able to make the width?

It can be seen, then, that show jumping is a far more complicated business than at first appears when we watch seemingly effortless performances by top-class riders, and we can begin to appreciate the hours of training which must go into the making of a first-class horse or rider.

The number of jumps included in a course must be not less than 10 for adult championship competitions, and not less than 7 for adult open competitions. If for some reason there are less than 7 obstacles on the course one at least must be jumped twice.

A clearly defined starting-line must be indicated by two flags or posts and, except in competitions where a timing device is used for the finish, there must also be finishing flags or posts. The starting line must not be more than 25 m (27 yd) and not less than 6.40 m (7 yd) from the first fence; and the finishing line must not be less than 15.54 m (17 yd) and not more than 25 m (27 yd) from the last fence. In an indoor arena the finishing line must not be less than 6 m (20 ft) from the last fence. Within these limits the length of a course varies according to the competition and the rules under which it is held.

SCORING TABLES, GRADING AND COMPETITIONS

International competitions open to international riders are judged according to the Fédération Equestre Internationale (F.E.I.) rules, and all others according to B.S.J.A. rules. The vast majority of competitions in Britain come under the latter ruling and are judged under 'Table A' or 'Table S'.

Table A is subdivided into A1, A2, A3 and A4 categories, which are always stated on the programme. Under Table A1, in the event of equality of faults for first place in the second jump-off, prize money is divided. Under 'A2' in the event of equality in the second jump-off, time is the deciding factor. Under 'A3' in the event of equality in the first jump-off, time decides. If there is still equality of faults and time (and the judge decides a further jump-off is essential), the final course must not exceed 6 obstacles. Under 'A4' time will decide for any award in the first round in the event of equality of faults. In the event of equality of time and faults the jump-off course must not exceed 6 fences.

Table S is used in competitions where time is the only factor. Penalties are converted into seconds, and 6 seconds are added to the total time taken for each obstacle knocked down. The time limit for these competitions is 2 minutes. The table for each competition is always shown in the catalogue.

Shows and competitions held under F.E.I. rules are subject to various complicated ratings. For the purposes of this book, however, it is sufficient to say they are classified as C.S.I.O. (Concours Saut International Officiel); C.S.I.E. (Concours Saut International Equipe); C.S.I. (Concours Saut International); C.C. (Concours Complet); C.C.I.

(Concours Complet International and relating to the Three-Day Event). The majority of international shows are held under the ruling of C.S.I.O. and C.S.I.

Each country (with one exception) may, under international rules, hold only one C.S.I.O. show each year. In Britain we hold the Royal International Horse Show as our C.S.I.O. show. Our other major international shows are held under C.S.I. rules. They include Hickstead (rated C.S.I.O. for the Nations Cup), Arena North, Windsor, Stoneleigh, Cardiff, Wembley (The Horse of the Year Show), and Olympia. The exception to the ruling for C.S.I.O. shows is America. It is the only nation which holds two C.S.I.O. shows in a year, one in Washington, the other in New York.

Only horses and ponies registered with the British Show Jumping Association are allowed to compete in shows affiliated to the association (and this virtually means every show except a few gymkhanas and small local shows), and both rider and owner must be members or junior members of the association. Registered horses are graded A, B or C according to the prize money they have won.

A Grade C horse does not, as many tend to think, imply an inferior animal, simply that the horse has so far won less than £150 in prize money. (At this stage it is also often referred to as a 'novice'.) Once its winnings reach £150 and until they reach £400, the horse becomes Grade B. Winnings of £400 and over put the horse in category A.

In the case of juniors the grading is different. A 'J.A' (Junior Grade A) pony is one which has won £75 or over, and a 'J.C' pony one whose winnings go from nothing to £75. With a few notable exceptions prize money is of course very much less in junior competitions, although there have been cases of a pony reaching 'J.A' in three shows by being amongst the winners at the few competitions where prize money goes up to £50 for the first prize. This is not a good thing for the pony, however, as it must lack experience, and will afterwards always have to compete against much more experienced and often older animals, and will tend to be overstrained.

There are numerous types of show jumping competitions, and when organizers draw up their programmes they try to include several different types in order to give variety and interest.

With one or two exceptions, the basic scoring is the same for all competitions (4 faults for a knock-down, 3 for a refusal, and so on), but each one is judged under a particular scoring table. The following gives a general outline of the B.S.J.A. rules governing the most popular types of competition.

Accumulator Competition   In this competition the course consists of between 5 and 7 obstacles, each bigger and more difficult than the one before. The first obstacle cleared scores 1 point, the second 2, and so on. No points or penalties are scored for a knock-down but a refusal means 3 penalty points, a second refusal 6, a third, elimination, and a fall of horse or rider 8 points as in other types of competition. A $\frac{1}{4}$ penalty point is incurred for each second taken over the time allowed which is calculated at 275 m (301 yd) a minute. The winner is the one with the highest score after deducting penalty points. If there is a tie, there is one jump-off against the clock over the whole course.

Area International Trials   These are confined to Grade A horses and must include a water jump. The object of the trials is to give selectors a chance to find horses of potential international material which may be able to go on to represent their country abroad as individuals or in Nations Cup teams. They are held annually in each county in Britain and are one of the qualifiers for the King George V and Queen Elizabeth II Cups.

Double Accumulator Competition This is really an extension of the single Accumulator, sometimes used when there are a large number of entries, or to make the competition run longer. It is jumped in two rounds, and the course consists of 7 obstacles. The first round collects points and penalties similar to those in the single Accumulator. Then approximately fifteen of the highest-placed riders qualify for the next round. In this no marks are scored for fences cleared, but the first one knocked down incurs 7 penalties, the second 6 and so on down to 1 penalty point for the 7th obstacle knocked down. The score of both rounds is worked out (penalties in the second taken off points gained in the first). Exceeding the time allowed is penalized by a $\frac{1}{4}$ penalty point for each second over. The time allowed is worked out at the same rate as for the single Accumulator.

Foxhunter Competition This competition is confined to registered horses in Grade C which have not won a total of £50 in jumping competitions. They must be ridden by adult members of the B.S.J.A. (Junior Foxhunter competitions are restricted to registered ponies which have not won a total of £35, owned by an adult and ridden by a junior member of the B.S.J.A.)

Gamblers Stakes Obstacles of varying heights are placed in the ring and on the wing of each is placed a large playing card. The more difficult the obstacle, the higher the value of the card, for example, an ace may count as 14 points, a king as 13, and so on down the line. The rider may choose any 7 obstacles and jump them in either direction. In a Multiple Gamblers Stakes Competition he may jump any obstacle as many times as he wishes; but in a 'Single', no obstacle may be jumped more than once. When he has jumped 7 obstacles he must leave the ring. As with a Scurry Competition two refusals or a fall do not count as they add to the time taken, which must not exceed 2 minutes. The winner is the one with the most points from the 7 jumps, in the fastest time.

Have a Gamble Stakes One of the most popular types of speed competition. The course consists of 12 to 14 fences each carrying a number of points relative to the severity of the fence. If the fence is jumped clear, the competitor scores the points value of that particular fence. He is allowed a time limit of 1 minute. Having jumped the first obligatory fence, the competitor may then jump any of the others in either direction and any order he likes, but he may not jump one fence more than twice. Fences are usually valued at 100, 90, 80, 70 and so on, down to 10 points. No faults are incurred for a knock-down but the competitor may not jump or attempt to jump that fence again. The winner is the one with the most points. If there is a tie, the course is unaltered, but competitors are allowed only 30 seconds to score.

High Jump Competition The jump must be constructed strictly in accordance with rules laid down by the B.S.J.A. and must be at least 6.10 m (20 ft) wide in front and must slope away from the direction in which the horse will approach. The horse must be given a ground line by filling in the space between the bottom pole of the jump with wattle hurdles or brushwood or some other type of fence to give an appearance of solidity. The jump usually starts at about 1.52 m (5 ft) in height and is usually raised 10.16 cm (4 in.) each time. The record officially recognized by the F.E.I. for a high jump is 2.29 m (8 ft 1½ in.) achieved in 1949 by a thoroughbred horse called Huaso, ridden by Capt. Alberto Larraguibel in Chile. The British record was set as far back as 1937 by Don 'Curly' Beard, riding a horse called Swank at Olympia. Swank cleared 2.29 m (7 ft 6¼ in.) and that record still stands. This competition is becoming increasingly rare and many people would like to see it abolished.

Hit and Hurry Competition Each competitor jumps the course in the correct order for 1 minute and gains 3 points for each obstacle jumped clear and 1 for any obstacle attempted but knocked down. First and second refusals or fall of horse and/or rider do not count as they serve to take up the time. When the time limit is reached, the bell is sounded and the competitor must cease jumping and go through the finishing line, which in this competition should be as near the centre of the ring as possible. If the Time Allowed expires during a refusal, the competitor must continue to attempt to clear the obstacle before crossing the finish. The winner is the one with most points, and if two are equal, time decides.

Hunting Competition This is sometimes described as a 'Scurry' and is basically a speed contest. No marks are given for faults made, but 6 seconds are added to the time taken by the competitor to complete the course for every obstacle knocked down, or for feet in the water. A fall or two refusals over the course do not count as these increase the time, but a third refusal means elimination. There is a time limit of 2 minutes and any competitor exceeding that time is disqualified. The winner is the rider with the fastest time.

Pair Jumping Competition In this type of competition, pairs of horses jump abreast and are judged as one for the purpose of faults. If both horses knock down an obstacle, only 4 faults are incurred, but if both horses refuse at the same fence, it counts as two refusals (and, as usual, the third refusal means elimination of the pair). If one horse falls behind the other, points are lost. 1 fault is counted for each length out of dressing[1] (but 4 faults at any one obstacle is the limit). Combination obstacles are not allowed in this type of competition.

Pair Relay Competition This is one of the most exciting competitions to watch. Two riders enter the ring together as partners. The first rider jumps the course and then passes his whip to the second rider who also jumps the course. It is a speed contest and the time is counted from when the first rider crosses the starting-line to when the second crosses the finish. If the first rider has three refusals or takes the wrong course, the judge's bell is sounded and the pair are eliminated.

Popular Open Competition This is open to all grades of horses owned and ridden by members of the B.S.J.A. which have not won a total of £300. (For Junior Popular Open the pony must not have won a total of £25 since being 'J.A'.)

Puissance Competition This type of competition is sometimes wrongly called a 'high jump', but spreads are included in the course though water and combinations are not allowed. The object is to test a horse's ability to jump wide as well as high obstacles. The height of the obstacles usually varies

---

[1] 'Out of dressing' means 'out of line abreast'. The term is a relic from the days when all show jumping was in the hands of the military. 'Dress by the right', for instance, means 'Get into a straight line'.

between 1.37 m (4 ft 6 in.) and 1.60 m (5 ft 3 in.), with the first obstacle slightly smaller to allow the horse to get into his stride. On a fence which is 1.60 m (5 ft 3 in.) high, the spread would probably be at least 1.80 m (6 ft). Those who tie for first place take part in a jump-off over a reduced number of fences which have been raised or widened. No less than 2 obstacles are allowed to remain on the course, and one of those must be a spread and one a straight obstacle (often a wall). When the height of the obstacle has reached 1.83 m (6 ft) or there have already been three jump-offs, those left in the competition may divide the prize.

Rescue Relay Competition   This is also a timed competition for two riders. The time limit must not exceed 2 minutes. Both riders enter the ring together, one going to the 'base' which is marked out somewhere on the course. He waits at the base until his partner has a fault (or a refusal or a fall). As soon as that happens the first rider must stop and the one at the base rides out and takes over the course at the fence following the one where the fault occurred. The first rider returns to the base and waits ready to rescue the second should he fault. If a competitor leaves the base without his partner having made a fault, the pair are eliminated. If the first rider has a clear round and there is still time left, the second rider starts off and jumps until the Time Allowed has expired. Points are awarded – 2 for each obstacle cleared and 1 for each attempted but knocked down – and the pair with the most points win.

Six Bars Competition   In this competition six 'bars' (sometimes the number is varied) which are upright obstacles are placed in a line with an equal distance between them. This distance is usually 9.35 m (30 ft 8 in.). It is usual for the obstacles to progress in height, but according to B.S.J.A. rules they may be all the same. The competition is judged under Table A of the rules (*see* p. 29) but it is not against the clock. If a rider knocks down a fence he continues to jump the remaining fences, but if his horse refuses or he (or the horse) falls, he must retake that fence.

In the second round only those riders with maximum points compete again, or those with equal lowest faults if there are no clear rounds. The heights of the bars are increased each round, but the competition must be ended after the fifth round even if there is still no decisive winner. In this rare case those who are still left in divide the prize.

Take Your Own Line Competition This is a speed competition in which no faults are given for fences knocked down, but 6 seconds are added to the time for every fence down and for feet in the water (if there is a water jump). Competitors may jump the obstacles in any order and from either direction, but must jump only once over each obstacle. The competitor with the fastest time wins. If a horse refuses, he must tackle the obstacle again from the same direction before going on to the next, and three refusals means elimination.

The Wing Newcomers Competition This is confined to registered horses in Grade C which have not won a total of £15, to be ridden by adult members of the B.S.J.A.

Timed Fault and Out Competition The course for this should provide a number of changes of direction to test the obedience of the horse and his skill in making a quick change, but combination obstacles are not permitted. Points are awarded instead of faults: 2 for each obstacle cleared. As soon as a horse knocks down a fence the judge's bell sounds. The competitor must then jump the next fence so that the time may be taken (no marks are awarded for this, but one is given for the fence knocked down) and leave the ring. The winner is the competitor with the most points in the fastest time.

BRITISH SHOWS

The two most important shows in Britain are both held in London, at Wembley. They are the Royal International Horse Show, the origins of which have already been discussed, and the Horse of the Year Show which is the big event in the autumn equestrian calendar.

It is at the Royal International that many of the major competitions in the show jumping world are staged. The most important of these is the team event for the Nations Cup (Prix des Nations) – held in 1975 at Hickstead as part of the Royal International Horse Show. Each country is allowed to stage only one Nations Cup competition each year, at its C.S.I.O. show. A team of four riders from each country jumps a usually formidable course twice and the best three scores count. According to international rules there must be at least three teams competing in a Nations Cup competition, which rules out certain parts of the world like Australia and New Zealand where distance and their quarantine regulations pose problems as yet unsolved. In the early days Nations Cup teams were almost always composed of cavalrymen, and back in 1931 the first British team ever to go to America consisted of the chief instructor of the Cavalry School at Weedon, Bede Cameron, Jack Talbot-Ponsonby of the 7th Hussars, Bobbie How of the 8th Hussars, and Mike Ansell of the Inniskillings. They competed against teams from Canada, Ireland, France and the U.S.A. – and they won the Cup.

In 1965 the Nations Cup events were given a fresh and exciting interest. The Duke of Edinburgh became president of the F.E.I., and he instituted a world team championship based on each country's best six Nations Cup results, and presented a cup, to be known as the President's Cup, for the winning country. In that first year it was won by Britain with a total of 35 points with Germany 4 points behind. Since then Britain has won it a further five times.

The points for the President's Cup are awarded according to the number of teams competing. For up to five teams the winner receives 5 points, for six teams they receive 6, and for seven or more they receive 7. The second team receives one less point, the third two, and so on down the scale.

At least six different riders must have represented their country in Nations Cup events during the year to make that country eligible. A nation cannot, therefore, send one brilliant team from competition to competition.

Of the world-famous individual championships the two most coveted of all are the King George V Gold Cup and the Queen Elizabeth II Cup, both held at the Royal International, the former restricted to men riders and the latter to women. In 1948 for the first and only time women were allowed to compete for the King George V Cup, and two women who did so were Pat Smythe on Finality and Lulu Rochford on Ladybird; they both got through to the final. The ladies' cup was presented by H.M. The Queen in 1949 when she was still Princess Elizabeth. It was known then as the Princess Elizabeth Cup, the name changing on her accession to the throne. The King George V Cup was given by that monarch in 1911 when it was won by a Russian. It was not competed for during the First World War or in 1919, and it was not until 1921 that a Briton won it for the first time – Lt-Col. Brooke on a horse called Combined Training. Four riders have won the cup three times each, Lt-Col. Jack Talbot-Ponsonby, Col. Harry Llewellyn and David Broome from Britain, and Col. Piero d'Inzeo from Italy. Only one horse has ever won it three times, the incomparable Foxhunter, ridden by Harry Llewellyn, the heroes of Britain's Gold Medal at the Helsinki Olympic Games.

There are strict qualifications of entry for both these championships. The only riders eligible are the previous year's winner riding the same horse; foreign riders who have been officially invited to compete at the show; members of the official British team for the show or those who have represented Britain in a Nations Cup competition since the previous Royal International Show; those who have been placed in the first six in an individual competition when representing Britain at a C.S.I.O. show; those who have won an Area International Trial in the year before the show.

Qualifications for entry for the Queen Elizabeth II Cup are slightly extended (largely because there are fewer top-class women riders) and includes any woman who has represented Britain at a C.S.I. (an official international) show abroad; a rider who is placed in the first two of an Area International Trial, and a rider who has been placed in the first three in certain Ladies Championship competitions throughout the year. This sounds a formidable list, but in effect the same people often qualify several times. In recent years, however, the number of qualifiers for the King George V Cup has often topped the 100 mark (110 in 1971, 132 in 1974) and the competition is divided into sections, with the leaders from each section competing for the final.

No one may ride more than one horse in either competition and every horse entered must be ridden by the rider who qualified it. So no one may buy their way into the championship by purchasing a horse which is qualified (always assuming the rather unlikely event of such a horse being for sale). On the other hand it is not uncommon for a rider to qualify more than one horse during the year, and then comes the all-important decision as to which horse to enter.

The other great Wembley show, the Horse of the Year Show, first started in 1949, but, like the Royal International, Wembley was not its original home. It started at the greyhound stadium at Harringay and for the first two years it was underwritten by the Greyhound Association. It moved to Wembley after ten years when the Harringay stadium was closed down, but its connections were for long recalled by the 'Harringay Spurs', presented to the rider gaining the greatest number of points with two horses during the week.

The idea of the show was conceived by the late Tony Collings who owned the Porlock Vale Riding School in Somerset and whose enthusiasm was fired by the success of an indoor show in Paris called 'Le Jumping'. Col. Sir Mike Ansell took over the organization of the show and with his tremendous flair realized that it must be a totally different affair from the Royal International if the public were to support it. So, as well as the competitions and show classes, he organized equestrian displays, the now famous Musical Drive of the heavy horses, the Horse Personalities of the Year parade, and the final Cavalcade on the last night. Nor have the juniors been left out. A feature of the show is the Mounted Games for the Prince Philip Cup (sponsored by the *Daily Mail*), which comprise exciting team events for youngsters from Pony Clubs all over Britain who have won their way through from an original entry of about 300 in preliminary and zone finals. Such has been the success of the Games that they have been taken up in Canada and America and the

F.E.I. has now included them in its list of International Rules.

But it is not only the Pony Clubs which must qualify to get to the Horse of the Year Show. Many competitions at the show are the 'finals' for those who have won at qualifying competitions throughout the country during the season. Some have fought their way to Wembley against opposition amounting to thousands. This is particularly true in the case of one of the oldest competitions of the show, which is now one of the largest single contests in the world, the *Daily Express* Foxhunter Novice Championship.

Named after Col. Harry Llewellyn's Foxhunter, the *Daily Express* competition was originally started by the London *Evening Standard* back in 1954 when the show was still at Harringay. The object was to encourage novice horses and owners, and the prize offered was the then enormous sum of £100. 'Foxhunter' classes were held at various shows and the winner of each came to Harringay to compete in the final. The competition snowballed. Show secretaries were inundated with entries (and were naturally delighted as they brought in extra entry fees), and often two competitions had to be run at a show. Interest became nation wide and the *Evening Standard* handed over the sponsorship to 'big brother', the *Daily Express*, which had a national circulation. Eventually regional finals had to be introduced and it is from the highest placed at these that the finalists for Wembley are selected. Many horses which have won this championship have gone on to international honours, for example, Beethoven (owned by Mr Douglas Bunn), the winner in 1962, who became World Champion when ridden by David Broome in 1970 at La Baule in France.

Some competitions at the show are entered direct, but even here there is a qualification as no horse may enter for Wembley unless it has won a certain sum of money during the season. The sum varies each year (it was up to £750 in 1975) but the amount is high, which means only the best and the experienced make it.

In some of the Horse of the Year classes foreign riders, who have been officially invited by the B.S.J.A. to compete, add an international flavour to the show and enable the public to see some of the best talent from abroad.

It is at the Horse of the Year Show that the contest for the coveted title 'Leading Show Jumper of the Year' (and in the younger ranks 'Leading Junior Show Jumper of the Year') is held. Entries for this class are restricted to the previous year's winner; those who have won a stipulated sum during the year; those who have been in official British Nations Cup teams or have been placed in the first six in international competitions at a C.S.I.O. show; and those placed first in various B.S.J.A. championships. So it will be seen that the winner really does have some claim to the title. The prize money is given by a sponsor. Those competing for the Junior title must qualify in earlier rounds. As in the case of the Pony Club Games this class is now sponsored by the *Daily Mail*, in partnership with Christy Beaufort, makers of safety riding hats.

The summer season is considered to be at an end after the Horse of the Year Show; and until recent years, the show marked the fall of the curtain for that year's sport. Now, however, there are so many enthusiasts that there is virtually a complete indoor winter season.

The highlight of the Christmas season in 1972, 1973 and 1974 was the Dunhill International Show at Olympia. Owing to the economic situation in 1975, the show was held with a number of different sponsors of whom Dunhills was one.

(*above*) The International Arena at Hickstead. A typical scene during a grand occasion: the start of the finals of the World Show Jumping Championship held at Hickstead for the first time in 1974. The four finalists line up behind the State Trumpeters.

(*below*) The show-ground of the Royal Windsor Horse Show in the Home Park at Windsor with the castle in the background. A British Driving Society meet is in progress.

(*above*) Part of the vast crowd at Hickstead watching an 'in-hand' parade of champions. These parades are sometimes held to give a break between show jumping competitions.

(*below*) The Cavalcade of Horses in the arena at Wembley which traditionally brings to an end the Horse of the Year Show.

The famous Derby Bank at Hickstead. The rider is Eddie Macken on Easter Parade.

All over the country indoor arenas have been built, most of them to full international specifications. The principal indoor centre is the National Equitation Centre at Stoneleigh, Kenilworth, Warwickshire, and it is here that many of the indoor championships are held. But many other indoor arenas have a regular programme, which consists of several meetings during the season and often includes an important championship. Harwood Hall at Upminster in Essex, where the Martell Championships are held, is an example. Other notable arenas include the Yorkshire circuit of the Lanni, Fulmer and Fielder arenas. At Park Farm, Northwood, Middlesex, the finals of the Lancia Competition are held early in the year, in which the first prize is a four-figure sum plus a new Lancia motor car. Qualifying classes for this competition are held at indoor arenas in many parts of the country. Park Farm also holds some of the Horse of the Year 'show' classes.

Many people still mourn the passing of the Royal International Horse Show from its outdoor setting at the White City to the indoor arena at Wembley. They feel that a city the size of London should be able to stage one big outdoor event in the classic manner. The difficulty is in finding a venue where not only the arena and the audience can be accommodated, but all the attendant cars, caravans and stables which must accompany a top-class show.

The Greater London Council does in fact stage a show on Clapham Common at the August Bank Holiday week-end. But although the show is growing and now extends over three days, and each year sees more of our top-class riders competing, it has some way to go before it could truthfully be bracketed with Wembley and Olympia.

Without doubt, show jumping's greatest outdoor arena in Britain is the All England Jumping Course at Hickstead in Sussex. Indeed, it is acclaimed as one of the greatest in the world by foreign as well as British riders.

Hickstead, through the medium of television, has brought show jumping to the millions as no other course has done. It is ideal for the cameras – out of doors, ornamental, with jumps of the toughest yet most interesting quality, both to rider and spectator. Douglas Bunn, the owner of Hickstead, is a perfectionist. Every pole is gleaming with new paint before each meeting, the greensward is meticulously tended so that the going is never less than excellent for the horses; and so for the spectators (and viewers) Hickstead presents a colourful spectacle, even before a horse enters the ring.

It was on 6th May 1960 that Douglas Bunn opened his All England Jumping Course in the grounds below his house, Hickstead Place. The début was an uncertain one. Bunn had decided to offer generous prize money in an effort to attract riders to try their luck at what was at that time a new-fangled adventure. But there were few willing to take up the challenge. Some were frankly scared at the continental type course, with its permanent fences, its water jumps, banks and tables.

But from the start, the Master of Hickstead, as he has come to be called since the phenomenal success of his venture, knew what he was about. He had been show jumping for years, starting as a junior in 1938, and after the war going on to senior and eventually to international events, all the time gaining ideas for what he would like to see at his own course. He knew what a horse was capable of jumping. He also knew that he did not want Hickstead to be just a rather attractive run-of-the-mill type course, but one which issued a real but fair challenge to horse and rider, and where winning would carry great prestige.

Ideas for Hickstead began to crystallize after Douglas Bunn watched the Men's European Championship at Aachen in West Germany in 1958 in which the Germans were 1st and 3rd. He realized then that the secret of continental success was not in the horses – Britain had just as good animals; nor the riders – the British were as brave and skilled; but in the fences and the way they were built. The fences on the Continent, especially in Germany, were big and solid with a lot of material in them. There were banks, there were tables, there were fences on different levels – and above all there was water, an endless variety of water. It was small wonder that our horses, when faced with this type of obstacle abroad, after the conventional and predictable poles and fences to which they were accustomed at most of the shows at home, should have difficulty in negotiating them. (Even so, Britain had had some great successes abroad, including winning the Gold Medal at the 1952 Olympic Games at Helsinki.)

Douglas Bunn was one of the first people to realize how much more could be built on Britain's earlier successes once similar continental type courses were introduced at home. All through the winter of 1959 he planned and worked on what is now the International Arena at Hickstead. Banks were thrown up, ditches dug, water jumps installed. Many of the obstacles constructed then were much as they are today. There was the Rotterdam Bank (since renamed the Irish Bank), the table, the road, the open ditch, the Devil's Dyke and the water jump, to mention a few.

The Derby Bank, which is among the most formidable and famous show jumping fences, came later, and is only used to its full awe-inspiring extent in the British Show Jumping Derby, which is

50

Hickstead's great classic contest and a major international jumping competition. Bunn got the idea for it while watching a newsreel in a Sussex cinema of the famous Hamburg Jumping Derby. Such a type of course with its huge Derby Bank as the predominating obstacle had never been seen in Britain. Bunn flew to Hamburg and, in the middle of a snowstorm, took measurements of every obstacle – height, width and distance apart. Then he returned to Hickstead and built his own Derby course making the Bank even higher than the German one at more than 3 m (actual height: 10 ft 6 in.). The Bank has an easy slope up, a small fence on the top, and then a precipitous drop at the far end, followed by a post and rail fence on the flat about two strides away. There are 16 fences on the course in all. The first Show Jumping Derby competition was held in 1961 and won by Irishman Seamus Hayes on Goodbye. Show jumpers come from all over the world to compete in this annual contest.

Naturally such a progressive and at that time revolutionary step in show jumping as the All England Jumping Course took cash as well as courage, and although Bunn had plenty of the latter, money presented a problem. A sponsor had to be found if Hickstead was to develop along the lines on which it had started.

Everyone who achieves success in their chosen field must at some time be given an element of luck. Douglas Bunn's came in 1961 when the tobacco firm of W. D. and H. O. Wills decided to sponsor Hickstead. They have remained loyal and generous throughout the years and in the world of sport their name has become as much associated with Hickstead as that of Douglas Bunn himself. It is thanks to them that Hickstead is now famous for the magnificent show-place that it is; with its coloured blocks of seats in the stands, its boxes reminiscent of Ascot, its spectacular International Arena, which without even a horse or a human being in it looks somehow brilliantly 'alive'; and above all for its international prestige among the cream of the world's show jumpers, all of whom have at some time ridden at Hickstead.

An important factor which has helped to make Hickstead a household word is that show jumping is a television 'natural'. The simple rules of today can be followed by every armchair viewer (the most important being four faults for a knock-down, three for a refusal, elimination for three refusals); its constant movement and the confined space of the arena make it an ideal sport for recording on the small screen.

Douglas Bunn foresaw the potential of television from the start, and as far back as 1963 Hickstead was being televised, at first by Southern Television, which covered the south coast from Dorset to Kent, with an occasional visit from the cameras of the national network of I.T.V.; and later, in 1971, Bunn signed a major contract with the B.B.C. who found the setting ideal, especially for colour television shots. The B.B.C. uses eight television cameras at Hickstead, and there are five permanent cable positions dug below the surface of the arena so that those cameras which are not set in permanent positions may be moved to cover the varying courses for different competitions.

The F.E.I. was not slow to recognize the quality of the arena at Hickstead or the evidence of ever increasing wins abroad at international shows by British riders, either as teams or individually, from 1960 on. These included two Olympic medals, two World Championships, numerous European titles, and the world team championship (for the President's Cup) several times. As far back as 1963 the F.E.I. approved Hickstead as the venue for the

Ladies European Championship (won by Pat Smythe on Flanagan in that year), followed two years later by the Ladies World Championship (won by Marion Coakes, now Mrs David Mould, on Stroller). There followed the Men's European Championship in 1969 (won by David Broome on Mister Softee) and in 1973 (won by Paddy McMahon on Pennwood Forge Mill), culminating with the Men's World Championship in 1974 (won by Hartwig Steenken of Germany on Simona). In addition two European Junior Team Championships have been held at Hickstead.

In 1971 the British Nations Cup contest (for the Prince of Wales Cup) was held at Hickstead – the first time it had been held out of London in its sixty-four year history. But because of what most people considered a petty insistence on a technicality by the Italians that the show was not the official British C.S.I.O., the win (by Britain) did not count towards the President's Cup and the competition was moved back to Wembley. In 1975, however, the July meeting at Hickstead became officially part of the International Horse Show, gaining C.S.I.O. rating and enabling Nations Cup competitions to be held out of doors with official recognition.

At the other end of the scale from the highest international competitions, Hickstead owes much of its fame and popularity to the way it caters for the junior show jumpers, those under 16, who are the nation's investment for the future of the sport. As has already been mentioned, European Junior Championships have taken place at Hickstead, and at every meeting there are competitions for juniors held every day in one or other of the 'outside' rings. Each competition is separate but usually also acts as a qualifier for a competition staged in the International Arena with a suitably modified course. This gives the youngsters not only the excitement and incentive to try their luck in that august enclosure, but also, at an early stage, vital experience of the feel of a great international ring, with crowds of spectators, and television cameras. Most of the major international shows in this country and the principal agricultural shows put on one junior event, but Hickstead is unique in its range of classes.

Yet at first Douglas Bunn was against including juniors in the programmes, and it was only the persistence of his brother George which made him relent in 1962. Many riders who have since won international fame started their careers in those outside rings at Hickstead, including Ann Moore, who went on to win an Olympic Silver Medal and become Ladies European Champion before she retired, and Debbie Johnsey, who became Junior Champion of Europe.

More recently, Douglas Bunn has introduced other equestrian classes to Hickstead and now there are show-rings for hunters, hacks, cobs and ponies. In 1974, at the spring meeting, he introduced a new and exciting cross-country team event, and once again showed his great flair for thinking up a hit for television. Many viewers declared they found this event even more exciting to watch than ordinary show jumping. There were teams of show jumpers, Event riders, jockeys, riders to hounds, riding clubs and cavalrymen. It was another 'first' for Hickstead.

Inevitably, following the phenomenal success of the All England Jumping Course, other permanent outdoor arenas have been built in various parts of the country. The most spectacular of these is Arena North which was first opened in June 1974 and provides a much-needed permanent show-ground for the north. This £3 million project at Charnock Richard in Lancashire was the brainchild of a young business man, John Rigby, from close-by Leyland. With the assistance of a young South African, Christopher Coldrey, he set out to provide a complete sports complex for the north of England, including a restaurant, a medieval banqueting hall, and motel. A huge outdoor arena was literally bulldozed out of the earth and tier upon tier of open seating built into the banks, in addition to covered seats and stands. The jumping course, built by Christopher Coldrey, is on a split level which gives it added spectator interest, and in places, where bushes and shrubs are growing, it resembles a cross-country course.

Unlike Hickstead, Arena North's inaugural meeting began in a spectacular fashion. Dunhills sponsored the new venture for its northern championships. All the top riders of Britain were there (it was to prove Ann Moore's last show before she announced her retirement and that of her great horse, Psalm), as well as all the top-ranking officials of the show jumping world. The weather conditions on the opening week-end, however, were appalling. The ground became so waterlogged with incessant rain that some of the competitions had to be abandoned, and the Dunhill Championship which had been planned as one of the most important competitions of the season, run as a Victor Ludorum over two different courses, was telescoped to a single-round competition. Because of the weather's effects on the going, the panel of judges exercised their prerogative and ordered one jump, which was sited on a bank with an unusual round-a-corner approach, to be moved after two riders had come to grief. (The riders were allowed to jump again.)

But these were teething troubles, aggravated by the weather. Since that first show junior and senior championships at national and international levels have been held at Arena North. Right from the start it was clear that this arena, young though it still is, will have the biggest impact on show jumping of any arena since the opening of Hickstead.

There are, springing up in different parts of the country, other permanent jumping courses, built to international requirements as regards the arenas, but at present not able to accommodate the large crowds which make up a great international show, although these new courses are beginning to play an increasingly important part in the show jumper's calendar. They are a significant pointer to the growing awareness of the value of having permanent arenas, built and designed for the sport, and which can therefore provide better built and more interesting obstacles and, most importantly, higher standards, which is essential if public interest in a sport is to be kept alive.

For hundreds of thousands of enthusiasts, however, their best opportunity to see top-class show jumping 'live' is to visit one of the great agricultural shows where many of the most important show jumping competitions form part of the programme. These shows, most of which now have their own permanent show-grounds, are run by the large agricultural societies, some of which, like the Bath and West, have been in existence since the 18th century, long before show jumping was ever thought of. But even in those far-off days there were classes for harness horses, hunters, heavy horses and breeding stock. After all, the horse was then the mainstay for transport and for working farm machinery, although a newspaper account of the show in Buckhurst Park on the borders of Kent and Sussex in 1838 records the fact that owing to insufficient entries the class for Ox Teams was cancelled, showing that in the very early days the horse did not have it all his own way.

These agricultural shows, which at one time had

relegated show jumping to a very minor place indeed, if they had not actually dropped it, now realize that thanks to Britain's increasing international success in the show jumping world, and the part television has played in popularizing this sport, it is about the biggest single crowd attraction. Sponsors, too, offer large sums in prize money, especially if their produce has some connection with the area, and this in turn ensures that leading riders and horses will compete.

Many of the country shows also provide a valuable field for novice horses (and often novice riders) to gain experience in some of the many classes that are held, usually in one of the outside rings where the limelight is not so strong. In these rings hundreds of young horses make their début in Foxhunter or Wing Newcomers classes. Junior riders have their own Foxhunter events.

Of the relatively few major shows which still cater solely for equestrian classes, without doubt the most important and prestigious is the Royal Windsor Horse Show, held early in the season, usually in May. The show was first started as an afternoon show by Mr Geoffrey Cross (who is now the chairman) in 1943. It was held then, as now, in the Home Park, Windsor, against the background of the castle. Soon after this first show, the Windsor Horse Show Club was formed and the Duke of Beaufort became its president, a position he still retains.

In 1944 King George VI and Queen Elizabeth visited the show and their two daughters competed in the single driving turn-out class. They were placed 3rd. King George VI became patron of the show (a position now held by his daughter, H.M. The Queen), and the show became the Royal Windsor Horse Show. In 1974 it was given C.S.I. status by the F.E.I. One of the major show jumping classes is the Ladies National Championship which has been held regularly at Windsor since 1971, having previously been held at different venues.

Until 1968 there also existed another big 'Royal' horse show – the Richmond Royal Horse Show, originally founded in 1892, and given 'Royal' status by Queen Victoria in 1897. In 1968, however, the show was incorporated into the South of England Show which had itself come into being as the show of the South of England Agricultural Society in 1967.

The South of England Show is held in June on the society's permanent show-ground at Ardingly, near Haywards Heath in Sussex. In 1974 H.M. The Queen visited the show and became its patron. The show lasts for three days and there is show jumping for most of the time in the outside rings. Principal competitions take place in the main ring and the most important of these is the Sussex Area International Trial which qualifies the winner to compete either for the King George V Gold Cup or the Queen Elizabeth II Cup at the Royal International Show.

Also in June – though often overlapping into July – is the Royal Show, the most important of all the great agricultural shows held in Britain. It is put on by the Royal Agricultural Society of England at its permanent show-ground at Stoneleigh in Warwickshire, which is also the head-quarters of the National Equestrian Centre. Until the society acquired the ground at Stoneleigh (the first show held there was in 1963), it had moved from venue to venue since its first show at Oxford in 1839.

In all there have been 136 Royal Shows held at places varying from Liverpool and Newcastle in the north to Windsor and Southampton in the south. Since moving to its permanent home at Stoneleigh it has acquired immense prestige. Its major show jumping classes are open to invited competitors and winners in the other rings only, and the sponsors of the classes give generous prize money.

Second only in size and older than the Royal Show is the Bath and West which is the show of the Bath and West and Southern Counties Agricultural Society, formed in 1777. It, too, now has a permanent show-ground, at Shepton Mallet in Somerset, and is busy preparing for its bi-centenary, in 1977. Prince Charles has accepted an invitation from the society to become president in that year.

The Bath and West, which holds its show in May, was one of the first shows to include show jumping as an attraction. In 1901 the show was held at Croydon and the catalogue of the time records: 'For the first time Jumping Competitions have been added to the prize list and there is a most satisfactory entry in these classes.' It went on to set down rules for the judge to follow, including taking into consideration 'the style in which the fences are jumped'.

In 1974 an important Welsh show jumping programme was launched, sponsored by the cigarette company, Benson and Hedges. This took place at Cardiff in the grounds of the castle and included an 'invited' championship for professional riders from home and abroad, and one for British and foreign amateurs, concluding with a match: professionals v. amateurs. The meeting was a great success and was repeated in 1975 at an earlier date than the previous year. As with many sporting activities sponsored by tobacco companies, the future is a little uncertain since much depends not only on the economic climate but on the law, which may be changed with regard to tobacco advertising.

In recent years there has been a marked upsurge

of interest in the art of dressage. Much of this interest has been kindled by the introduction of 'Dressage with Jumping' competitions in which horses are required to perform a dressage and a show jumping test only. These competitions are held in various parts of the country at horse shows rather than at Horse Trials. One firm sponsors a series which culminates in the winners competing for a championship at the Horse of the Year Show each year.

Just to complicate things for the spectator, the dressage tests in Dressage with Jumping competitions at many county shows are marked on a system of 'good' points instead of penalty points, so that the rider with the highest score after the dressage is in the lead. The jumping is then marked on a series of 'penalty' points which have to be subtracted from the dressage score to decide the ultimate winner.

From time to time there have been moves to bring the system of scoring for this type of competition and for Eventing under one rule, for even the riders themselves have been known to get muddled. So far nothing has come of it, but life would be simplified if the bodies concerned would agree on a universal formula for marking.

PRINCIPAL OVERSEAS SHOWS

Show jumping is one of the most international of sports, and in Europe and across the Atlantic in America and Canada there are many important shows.

Although the British Show Jumping Derby at Hickstead has now become the great classic competition of the sport, the idea was first thought of in Hamburg and the Hamburg Derby is still one of the most sought-after competitions to win. It is held every year early in June. More than fifty years ago an enthusiast called Herr Pulvermann had the idea of a Show Jumping Derby and one of the fences on the course is named after him. The Derby Bank in Hamburg is, according to those who have jumped both, a softer descent than that at Hickstead.

The Germans have always been enthusiastic show jumpers and Germany was among the original countries to become affiliated to the F.E.I. in 1921. After the Second World War the East German Federation was formed in 1965 and was recognized by the F.E.I.

The principal show in Germany is held at Aachen in West Germany and is a C.S.I.O. show. It is usually held at the end of June or beginning of July and is one of the biggest horse shows in the world. It attracts the crack riders from most countries, who face stiff opposition from the home side, for they are among the world's best riders.

Another of the great European shows is the Rome show, for the Italians are also a great riding nation. Rome is the Italian C.S.I.O. show and it is held in the beautiful Piazza di Siena, which has often earned it the title of the most beautiful horse show in the world. It is one of the earlier shows of the season and is usually held early in May. In 1969 the Italians also started a Jumping Derby and this is held at Olgiata about 15 miles outside Rome. The Italians hold a number of other important shows, the most notable being at Venice and Naples. Italy was another of the original member countries of the F.E.I. in 1921.

France has always been one of Europe's leading equestrian nations and was also an original member of the F.E.I. There are numerous important shows during the season in France to which competitors from many countries travel to compete. The most notable are held in Paris, Nice, Dinard, Fontaine-bleau and La Baule, the latter being the venue for the World Championships in 1970. The big Paris show, like the Wembley Horse of the Year Show, is an indoor show. It is held in mid-winter, in December. There is also a spring show in Paris. The French C.S.I.O. show is held at Fontainebleau, 37 miles south-east of Paris, a favourite summer resort with its historic palace and famous forest. The show is held in midsummer in June.

Lisbon, Rotterdam, Barcelona, and Ostend are all C.S.I.O. shows for their particular countries and competitors from many nations travel to them, especially when the pressure is on in the battle for the President's Cup for the nation gaining the most points in Nations Cup competitions. Lisbon especially is a great favourite for picking up points as it is held towards the end of the season, late in September, by which time the pattern is beginning to emerge. However, the final analysis of positions is often not known until after the great shows of the North American circuit.

The United States, which first introduced show jumping competitions into its New York Horse

Show programme as far back as 1909, was also one of the original members of the F.E.I. in 1921. The Americans are tremendous show jumping enthusiasts and often travel the European circuit. They first competed in Britain in 1910 when the International Horse Show was held at Olympia.

The three major U.S. horse shows are all held indoors. They are at Washington, Harrisburg and New York, and both Washington and New York count as C.S.I.O., for although in other cases each country is allowed only one C.S.I.O. show, America may hold two since she covers such a large area. All three shows are held in October and November.

The most famous American Show is the New York Show which takes place in Madison Square Garden, where the first horse show was held in 1883. The show became international in 1909 when the then U.S. President, Alfred Vanderbilt, who took a great interest in equestrian affairs, suggested that foreign competitors should be invited, and a number of British riders crossed the Atlantic to compete as individuals.

The United States does not have an equestrian federation of its own as do most other countries, but its internal show jumping affairs are administered by the American Horse Shows Association. The official headquarters for training equestrian teams is at Gladstone in New Jersey and there are two official trainers. At present they are Bertalan de Nemethy for show jumping and Jack le Goff for Eventing.

Canada came somewhat later into the full-scale show jumping world, for the Canadian Horse Shows Association was not formed until 1946 and it was not until four years after this that they became affiliated to the F.E.I. However, their famous show held at the Royal Winter Fair in Toronto has attracted international show jumpers from both sides of the Atlantic for more than thirty years. Although they may have been slower to start, the Canadians lost no time in making up for lost ground, and in 1968 they won the Olympic Gold Medal for the team show jumping event in Mexico.

As almost every country throughout the world has at some time gone to Ireland for Irish-bred horses, it would be wrong to end this chapter without mentioning the Dublin Horse Show (C.S.I.O.) which takes place at Ballsbridge early in August and attracts riders and spectators from all over the world. Without doubt the Irish were the first to introduce any form of show jumping into their horse show programmes, for in 1865, when the show was held in Kildare Street, 'leaping' competitions consisting of two 'leaps', a high and a wide, were introduced to test a horse's suitability for the hunting field.

HORSE TRIALS OR EVENTS

Modern Horse Trials, also termed 'Events', are a development of 'The Military'[1] as the sport was known earlier in the century, when it consisted of simple tests and long-distance rides designed to test the fitness of officers and their chargers. Today in Britain Horse Trials come under the aegis of the British Horse Society which was founded in 1947 by the amalgamation of the Institute of the Horse and Pony Club with the National Horse Association of Great Britain. It lays down the rules and sets the standards for every phase of Eventing, which is one of the fastest-growing branches of equestrianism and very popular as a spectator sport. The B.H.S. also keeps a watchful eye on all matters relating to horses and their welfare in Britain.

Horse Trials started in Britain with Three-Day Events, modelled on the Olympics, Badminton being the pioneer. Indeed the major international competitions are still carried out over a full three-day period. These include Badminton, Burghley and the European and World Championships, and some major Events abroad, such as Boekelo in Holland, Mölbling in Austria, Kalmthout in Belgium and Ledyard Farm in the United States. As the popularity of the sport has grown in this country, other suitable places to hold Trials have had to be found. Often the landowners (who are in many cases the organizers also) do not have the facilities or the space to hold a Three-Day Event, neither is every horse and rider keen to take part up to the standard of a full-scale competition. (It

---

[1] Still known as the 'militaire' on the Continent.

would be like compelling every keen club cricketer to take part in test matches.) So there has grown up in Britain a network of Two- and One-Day Events – and excellent proving grounds for higher things they have become, so much so that the British Horse Society now insists that horses must have had a certain amount of experience in these before moving on to the more important Trials. But the basic object of all Horse Trials is the same – to prove the obedience and suppleness, the courage, speed and endurance, and the fitness of the horse.

Obedience and suppleness are proved by dressage tests; courage, speed and endurance by covering miles of roads and tracks, jumping a steeplechase course, and a cross-country course with anything up to thirty or more jumps; fitness, by the final day's ability to complete a normal show jumping course. The tests are scaled down and parts often omitted altogether in the One- and Two-Day Trials, but the dressage, cross-country, and show jumping basic phases remain.

Dressage – the first day's test – is probably the most difficult for the spectator to follow, and from the point of view of sheer spectacle the least interesting. Yet it is the basis of all horse training, for as the most exalted prima ballerina does her barre practice to keep her muscles supple and co-ordinated, so dressage gives a horse balance and suppleness, and trains him in obedience, and the execution of all movements with lightness and grace and seeming effortlessness. The whole object of the Dressage Test in Horse Trials is to ascertain the level and quality of a horse's education and to test the complete obedience of the horse under the control of the rider who must rely entirely on his seat, hands, and legs for guiding the horse. Any verbal aid or clicking of tongue is severely penalized. Dressage can best be described as a series of drill exercises ranging in

66

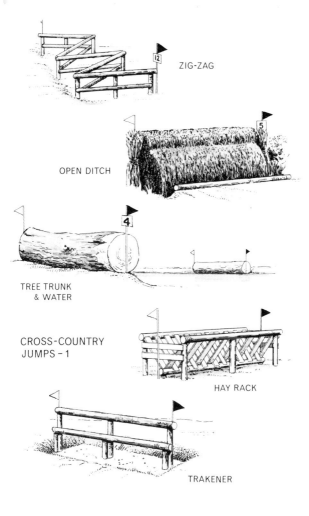

ZIG-ZAG

OPEN DITCH

TREE TRUNK
& WATER

CROSS-COUNTRY
JUMPS – 1

HAY RACK

TRAKENER

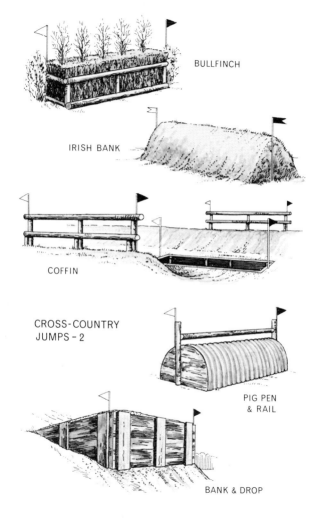

BULLFINCH

IRISH BANK

COFFIN

CROSS-COUNTRY
JUMPS – 2

PIG PEN
& RAIL

BANK & DROP

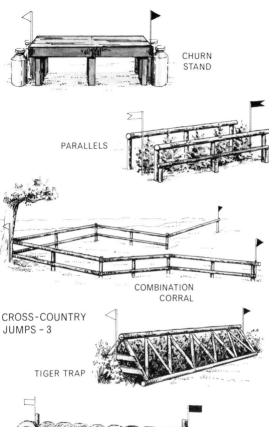

CHURN STAND

PARALLELS

COMBINATION CORRAL

CROSS-COUNTRY JUMPS – 3

TIGER TRAP

TYRES

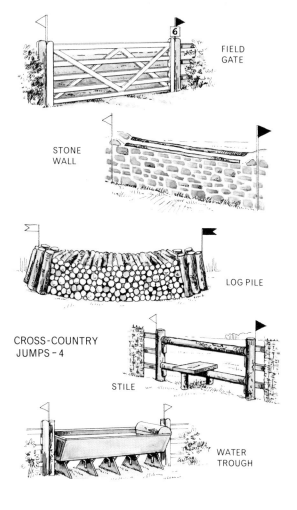

FIELD GATE

STONE WALL

LOG PILE

CROSS-COUNTRY JUMPS – 4

STILE

WATER TROUGH

severity according to the standard of the competition. A test can involve up to twenty different movements. The names of many of these movements show the influence of the great continental schools – *appuyer*, *volte*, *pirouette*, *renvers*, *passage*, *piaffe*, and so on. Some of these of course occur only in the most advanced type of dressage and would not be required in a test included as a phase of an Event.

The history of dressage goes back to the days when horses were man's sole support in battle. Many of the movements have their origin in the tactics necessary for survival against a foe either on foot or on another horse. They included kicking out both back legs together (to fell a man creeping up at the rear or to maim another horse), rearing on the hind legs (to avoid a knife or sword aimed to maim the horse or bring down the rider), or even to leap clean into the air (to clear an enemy lying in wait on the ground). Many of these movements still survive in the 'Haute Ecole' of the Lippizaner horses at the Spanish Riding School in Vienna, but otherwise have been much modified even for the most advanced tests.

For many years on the Continent dressage has been a most important part of equestrianism, evolving from the great riding schools in Vienna, France, Italy and Spain. In recent years the British and Americans have also started to take dressage as a separate and serious art (aided in Britain by substantial sponsorship by John Pinches for international dressage championships held at Goodwood). The standard for this type of dressage is high and is laid down by the F.E.I. It includes the Prix Saint Georges Medium Standard; the Reprise Intermediaire of Advanced Standard, and the Grand Prix of Olympic Standard. These very high standard tests are not used in Eventing even for international Three-Day Event championships

(C.C.I. and C.C.I.O.).

The test used for international Three-Day Event championships is the F.E.I. Concours Complet test. (Badminton and Burghley are examples.)

For One-Day, Two-Day and standard Three-Day Events (Tidworth is an example of the latter), B.H.S. tests are used. Occasionally in an Advanced Two-Day Trials the F.E.I. test is imposed. If this is not used, the B.H.S. Elementary dressage test is chosen. The Elementary test is also used for an Advanced Class One-Day Trial.

British Horse Society tests are graded as follows: 1–10 Preliminary Standard; 11–20 Novice Standard; 21–30 Elementary Standard; 31–40 Medium Standard; and 41–50 Advanced Standard. There are special tests for Pony Clubs, and the F.E.I. also lays down special tests for junior international Events.

Tests must be ridden individually and there are definite rules for the size of the arena. It must be rectangular, 60 m × 20 m (198 ft × 66 ft); or 40 m × 20 m (132 ft × 66 ft). Tests below Medium Standard are normally held in the smaller arena. The course which the rider must take is clearly marked out by letters and the course varies according to which test is being taken.

Judging is carried out by a panel of three judges (in a small One-Day Trial there is often only one) and the scoring is by a system of penalty points so that the rider with the lowest score wins. In a dressage competition which is not part of an Event, the highest score wins.

The Speed and Endurance Test takes place on the second day of a Three-Day Event and is divided into four phases. Phases A and C consist of Roads and Tracks – anything from 9–19 km (6–12 miles) – which must be covered at a stipulated pace, usually faster than a trot and not so fast as a canter. Phase B is the Steeplechase course, with about 12 fences, which must again be completed in a given time usually necessitating riding at a gallop. Although the Roads and Tracks may seem uninteresting to the spectator, these are the basis of the test of endurance. During Phase C a rider will often dismount and run beside his horse to give the animal a breather after the Steeplechase. At the end of these three phases there is a compulsory halt of 10 minutes during which a vet examines each horse to see if he is fit to undertake the fourth phase, the Cross-country, which is the kernel of all Trials and the chief attraction for the thousands of people who flock to them every year. (At Badminton 130,000 or more people usually visit the Three-Day Event.)

The Cross-country phase varies from just over 5–8 km (3–5 miles) in length and includes between 30 and 40 obstacles, solidly built to represent as far as possible the natural obstacles which might be met across country, often including big drops, and sometimes involving several jumps to clear one obstacle, so that in 35 fences a horse may leave the ground more than 40 times. The course is marked by flags and the rider must go between these. Around each obstacle is an area known as the penalty area, again clearly defined by flags, and faults are incurred only if they occur within this area.

Any outside assistance, given anywhere on the course, to a rider or horse, or any intervention by a third party, even if unasked, with the object of aiding either horse or rider means immediate disqualification. There have, for instance, been cases where a rider was about to take the wrong course when a well-meaning outsider, shouting to him to put him right, has instead cut him out of the competition. The only exception to this rule is when a rider falls, then he is allowed help to adjust his saddlery or to remount, or in catching the loose horse.

On the final day there is another veterinary inspection of the horses and any which appear injured, lame, or over fatigued from the previous day are not allowed to continue. It says much for the training and care given to British horses that only a very few fail this test of those that have managed to get round the cross-country course, which of course many fail to do, either falling, refusing three times, or taking a wrong course.

The third and final day's test is the Show Jumping. This is over a normal show jumping course of 10 or 12 obstacles which must be covered in a given time. By show jumping standards it is not severe but often proves the decisive factor when the scores are very close after the first two days.

There can never be a dead heat in a Three-Day (or any smaller) Event. If two or more competitors have the same marks when all three days' scores are added together, the first place goes to the one with the fastest time in the cross-country. In the highly unlikely event of this still producing a tie, the fastest time on the steeplechase is taken into account. All phases are marked on a penalty-points basis, the winner being the competitor with the lowest score.

Scoring in an international Three-Day Event

First refusal, run-out,[1] or circle of
   horse at an obstacle: 20 penalties

Second refusal, run-out, or circle of
   horse at the same obstacle: 40 penalties

[1] A 'run-out' occurs when a horse tries to avoid an obstacle to be jumped by running out to one side or the other.

Third refusal, etc. at the same obstacle:	eliminated
First fall of horse and/or rider at obstacles in the Steeplechase or Cross-country phase:	60 penalties
Second fall of horse and/or rider at obstacles during the Steeplechase phase:	eliminated
Second fall of horse and/or rider at obstacles during the Cross-country phase:	60 penalties
Third fall of horse and/or rider at obstacles during the Cross-country phase:	eliminated
Omission of obstacle or red or white flag:	eliminated
Retaking an obstacle already jumped:	eliminated
Jumping an obstacle in the wrong order:	eliminated

Penalty points are also incurred for exceeding the 'Time Allowed' for the different phases – Roads and Tracks, Steeplechase, and Cross-country. On the Roads and Tracks 1 penalty point is added for each second over the Time Allowed, up to the time limit, which is one-fifth more than the Time Allowed (i.e. if the Time Allowed is 5 minutes, the time limit would be 6 minutes). Any competitor who exceeds the time limit is eliminated.

On the Steeplechase 0.8 of a penalty point is added for each second in excess of the Time

Allowed up to the time limit, which is twice the Time Allowed. Exceeding the time limit means disqualification.

The penalty for every second taken in excess of the Time Allowed on the Cross-country phase is 0.4 of a penalty point up to the time limit, which is based on a speed of 225 m (246 yd) a minute. For example, if the course is 7,200 m (7,874 yd) and the Time Allowed is 12 minutes 38 seconds, the time limit is 32 minutes.

No bonus points are gained by taking less than the Time Allowed for each phase. This removes any temptation for riders to over-push their horses.

In the Show Jumping phase of the Trial, the marking is different from that of ordinary show jumping, and is as follows:

First refusal:	10 penalties
Knocking down an obstacle:	10 penalties
Touching a boundary mark, or feet in the water or in the ditch:	10 penalties
Second refusal in the whole test:	20 penalties
Third refusal:	eliminated
Jumping an obstacle in the wrong order:	eliminated
Error of course not rectified:	eliminated
Fall of horse or rider:	30 penalties

There are also penalties for exceeding the Time Allowed – a $\frac{1}{4}$ penalty point for every second up to the time limit.

The speed required varies according to the class of the Trial, as indeed does the system of judging the Roads and Tracks, Steeplechase and Cross-country. The tables in the foregoing lists apply to the highest class of full Three-Day Events, such as Badminton, where the horses competing are in the Advanced and International classes, or at Burghley, where both the European Championships and the World Championships have been staged. Scoring for One- and Two-Day Events, or for those held as 'standard' Three-Day Events such as Tidworth, are on a less severe scale.

From the foregoing account of what is asked of a horse in a Three-Day Event, it is obvious that only the very top-class horses take part, and no horse is likely to compete in more than two such Events in a year.

Because of the difficulty in finding suitable space, not only to organize a full Three-Day Event for competitors but also to accommodate thousands of cars and spectators, there are a very limited number of Three-Day Trials. As in show jumping, the F.E.I. allows only one official Trials for each country (a Concours Complet International Officiel Trial). Burghley receives this rating when European or World Championships are held there. At other times, as at Badminton, it rates as a C.C.I. (Concours Complet International) Trial.

At Bramham Park in West Yorkshire there is now a 'standard' Three-Day Event organized at the end of September in the beautiful grounds of the Queen Anne house originally built for the first Lord Bingley, 5 miles from Wetherby Racecourse, where the horses competing are stabled.

At Tidworth in Hampshire the Army organizes a Three-Day Event in the spring (usually in May) which is largely supported by civilians. Indeed so great has the entry list been in recent years that it is now divided into four sections. The Trials are graded as 'standard' and prove an excellent stepping-stone for horses, giving them a chance to get used to the demands of a Three-Day Event before tackling the rigours of a full international competition such as Badminton or Burghley. Tidworth also puts on a full-scale Trials for juniors.

The other Three-Day Event held in Britain is at Wylye on Salisbury Plain, on the estate of Lord and Lady Hugh Russell. Lord Hugh is tremendously enthusiastic and has often competed in Horse Trials. Wylye is usually held at the end of September or early in October. The setting at Wylye has the great advantage that from the summit of the hill, where the control centre, refreshment tents, score boards and trade stands are located, spectators can see almost all the course and follow the progress of the riders in the cross-country phase.

By far the majority of Event horses compete in One- or Two-Day Trials. Most Horse Trials in Britain – and there are more than sixty held in a season – are One-Day Events. These consist of a dressage test, show jumping, and a cross-country course (much shorter and with considerably less formidable obstacles than for the Three-Day Events), and no steeplechase or roads and tracks phases. The show jumping is often held before the cross-country phase which is more convenient for organizers and competitors. All Trials start with the Dressage Test, however, as it would not be fair to expect a horse to give a flowing, balanced performance when tired and 'blown' after a cross-country ride.

Horses which compete in any Trials must be registered with the British Horse Society (in the same way as show jumpers must be registered with the British Show Jumping Association) and are graded I, II, or III according to the number of points they have built up in different categories of competition.

The Trials are also graded according to the

difficulty of the tests imposed – Advanced, Intermediate or Novice. Novices are those with less than 10 points; Intermediate with 10–30; Advanced are those with 31 or more points. Sometimes a Trial may have classes for two or all three grades, with varying dressage tests and obstacles on the cross-country course, suitable for each grade of horse.

In order that the very top-grade horses should not be overtaxed on the one hand, nor have too few competitions available to them, many Trials have what is known as an 'Open Intermediate' class. This means that although the course is categorized as Intermediate (which most are, as few organizers have the course builders or the facilities for a full advanced course), a Grade I horse may enter. This is the only situation in which a horse is allowed to compete in a lower category than that of his official grading.

Before every Trial an official steward appointed by the British Horse Society must inspect and pass the course as appropriate for the particular competition, and must remain there to see that the rules are correctly interpreted, adjudicate in any dispute, and be available to interpret the rules if there is any query on the part of competitors or organizers.

Horse Trials fixtures are divided into two seasons: spring and autumn. The spring season goes roughly from March till May and the autumn from August to October. This enables horses to be turned out for the summer to enjoy the summer grass, or to take part in the hunting season. Without entering into any controversy as to the desirability or otherwise of hunting, many leading riders say it is the best possible way to get a horse fit for Trials, and one of the most valuable ways for a rider to gain experience in all types of cross-country obstacle.

It says much for the healthy state of the sport that every week during the season there is at least one – and often two or three – Trials taking place in different parts of the country. Considering how much land must be made available even for a One-Day Event, and the organization necessary for building fences, arranging stabling and car parking, recruiting voluntary stewards and judges (the latter must of course be qualified), and checking entries and working out results, it can be seen just what enthusiasm this sport arouses.

Princess Anne's participation and success in the sport, and her marriage to another leading rider, Capt. Mark Phillips, who was in the successful Olympic team at Munich and the World Championship team at Punchestown in 1970, have played a great part in the tremendous growth in its popularity. The sport suddenly became 'news' and millions of people crowded to their nearest Trials ground or to their television screens to find out what it was all about. H.M. The Queen has been a keen follower since the early 1950s.

Another reason for the popularity of Horse Trials is that the onlooker can take a much more active part than is usual in many sports. During the cross-country phase he can walk from one jump to another, following the course, and comparing the way the horses tackle the fences. Indeed, the enthusiastic follower will find he also has to be pretty fit, as he will cover anything up to 8 or 9 km (5 or 6 miles) on some courses. Experienced spectators say the best way to follow the course on foot is to start at the last fence and work backwards. By doing that you will be facing the oncoming horses and are less likely to get in the way, but it also shortens the waiting time between each horse arriving at a fence. The horses start off at 5-minute intervals, and mounted stewards on the course blow whistles to warn onlookers of the approach of a competitor.

As most Horse Trials are held in parkland on private estates, even those visitors who know – or even care – little about the rules of the sport find they have an excellent day out in the country, usually with a family picnic, and an opportunity for some exercise. Indeed, it is in this way that thousands of the keenest spectators have been recruited. They came for a picnic, they decided after all to find out what it was all about – they were hooked!

Eventing is still one of the most truly amateur sports, and Horse Trials are organized almost entirely on a voluntary basis. The big Three-Day Events are an exception. They need a full-time staff for many months of the year to deal with all the applications from abroad, the qualifications for entry, the entries, accommodation, stabling, and so on. The technical assistants, such as course designers and scorers provided by the British Horse Society, are paid at all Trials but most of the judges, stewards, timekeepers, runners,[1] secretaries and the host of others involved all give their services free.

It does, however, cost a great deal of money to put on even a One-Day Trial. There is the hiring of tents, printing of programmes, score sheets, etc., loudspeakers, the labour for building the course, the hire of jumps for the jumping phase, and so on. Then too there must be the chance of a reasonable return in prize money if riders are to bring horses a long distance with the present costs of upkeep and transport.

Badminton and Burghley Horse Trials were lucky in finding commercial sponsors early on, for

[1] 'Runners' are usually members of the local Pony Club who carry score sheets (or messages) from individual judges (either at dressage rings or far out on the course at each fence) back to the main control post so that overall scores and placings may be worked out and posted on the results board.

the enormous publicity these Trials receive give a fair return for their investment. Handsome prizes are offered – essential for a big international event. In 1974 Whitbreads gave the record sum of £1,000 first prize to the winner of Badminton in addition to the magnificent trophy they had given for years. Raleigh are the sponsors of Burghley.

For the smaller Trials the story was different. Most of them could only rely on local sponsorship, probably from a local firm or shop, and looked to admission money to meet most of the costs. With the vagaries of the British climate, especially in spring and autumn, this often spelt disaster, and for a time it looked as if the One-Day Trial, which is the backbone of the sport, might become another financial casualty. Then along came the biggest shot in the arm that any sport could have asked. In 1969 the Midland Bank took over the sponsorship of every official B.H.S. Horse Trial in the country, not already covered by a sponsor of its own. With its associate banks, Clydesdale and Northern, helping out in Scotland and Ireland, the Midland Bank provides prize money, advertising and publicity in general.

The Midland Bank also initiated the National Championships of Great Britain both for Novice and Open classes. For these the winners of each class at every Horse Trial are eligible, plus, in the Open division, those who have competed in international events. The championships are held in the autumn each year, and in addition to good prize money the winners each receive a trophy which is held for a year – the Golden Griffin Trophy for the Novice class and the Golden Griffin Plate for the Open.

The overall effect of this sponsorship has been a very happy one. It has made it possible for the smaller Trials to continue in business, rather than adding to the spoils of the fortunate few, and it is these smaller Trials which are the nursery of the sport and from which the great international winners eventually emerge.

As in show jumping, the term 'novice' applies strictly to the horse – there is no penalty for a world champion riding in a novice Trial. Indeed, Mary Gordon-Watson, the 1970 World Champion, frequently brings out a new young horse at a small One-Day Trial, as do other champions and Olympic medallists.

The building and designing of a cross-country course, be it for novices or the very highest international class, is an art in which few people excel. The British Horse Society has a panel of expert course builders for Eventing, as the B.S.J.A. has for show jumping. If for any reason one of the official panel is not employed to build the course, it must be passed by a steward of the British Horse Society before it can be used in an official competition. The B.H.S., unlike the B.S.J.A., does have a scheme for training builders for cross-country courses. Two of the leading course builders in this country are Bill Thomson, a qualified veterinary surgeon who has been technical adviser to the B.H.S. for more than twenty years, and former European Champion, Col. Frank Weldon, who builds the course at Badminton. Bill Thomson designs the course at Burghley for the Three-Day Event Championships and for the World and European Championships when they are held there.

Unlike show jumping, there is not the same rigid set of rules in the design of a cross-country course nor is the course contained in a given space. It may stretch across downs, farmland, fenland, moors, wooded uplands, plains such as the course at Wylye across Salisbury Plain, or scrub-covered heath like that at Crookham in Hampshire. The art is to assess what a horse, according to its grade, may be expected to jump with a fair chance of success. The course must take into account and put to best use any natural obstacles which may be encountered, for example, the quarry or the lake at Badminton, or the trout hatchery at Burghley.

Most people who have never ridden a cross-country course, or indeed taken a horse over any kind of jump, find it difficult to realize that the more massive and solid and apparently unbreakable the fence, the more inviting it will be to a well-trained, fit, bold horse. Yet, at the same time, the course designer must pay great attention to the safety aspect. However solid the fence may appear, if there are casualties, it is essential that the horse or rider may be quickly extricated; there must be no jagged edges, nails, or, above all, wire, which could rip and wound a horse; and at every jump there must be easy accessibility in case there is need of a stretcher for a fallen rider. Fortunately, there is seldom a really bad fall in spite of the hair-raising appearance of many of the jumps. Indeed, most of the experienced riders say the terrifying-looking jumps are often the ones which the horse takes most easily in his stride.

It is often wondered why Badminton, such an important and renowned course, is not chosen as the venue for international championships. In the early days of the sport, when the first European Championships were held in 1953, they were staged at Badminton – and would have been again in 1955 had H.M. The Queen not offered to lend Windsor Park for the event. But, unfortunately, the spring proved a bad time to stage an international event. Many of the European countries experience much harder winters than we do, and spring comes later, therefore they do not have the time to get their horses fit after the winter lay-off. So when international championships are to be held in Britain, they now take place in the autumn at the Burghley Three-Day Event; formerly they were held at Harewood.

Since the early days of Badminton Britain has achieved tremendous success internationally. British teams have won the Gold Medal at the Olympic Games three times (1956, 1968 and 1972). In 1972 Richard Meade won the Individual Gold Medal and in 1956 Frank Weldon won the Bronze, while Derek Allhusen won the Silver in 1968. Britain won the World Championships in Ireland in 1970, both for the team and the individual title (Mary Gordon-Watson took this). Britain has won the European Championship seven times (1953, 1954, 1955, 1957, 1967, 1969, 1971), and eight British riders, including Princess Anne, have won the Individual European Champion title.

In an international team event, including the Olympics, four riders are usually nominated, and at the end, the best three scores count. If one member of the team is eliminated, the other three may carry on; but if, as sometimes happens, a country is only able to nominate three riders, all three must finish the course. It was this rule which spurred on Janet Hodgson of the British team in the European Championships at Kiev in 1973. In spite of two terrible falls and severe facial injuries, she carried on to finish the cross-country course and keep Britain in the race. One member of the team was already out, but thanks to Janet, the British stayed in and won the Bronze Medal.

In addition to its team members, each country is allowed to enter a specified number (always very limited) of individual riders who compete solely for the individual prize. Often this will be a brilliant young rider whom the selectors feel has not had enough experience to sustain the added strain of being part of a team with all its responsibility. It was when she was nominated as an individual for her first international championship Event that Princess Anne became European Champion at Burghley in 1971, a few weeks after her 21st birthday. She was riding the ill-fated but brilliant Doublet, who was to die so tragically in 1974 when he broke a leg while the princess was exercising him in Windsor Park.

Most of the principal Three-Day Events overseas occur during the summer, just when the British riders count on allowing their horses to have their summer 'let-down'. On the Continent many horses have one continuous season from early summer to late autumn, instead of the two almost separate seasons enjoyed in Britain. This could make it difficult for British riders to compete, but most of those interested in riding abroad manage either to keep a horse in training just a little longer after the spring programme, resting him further into the autumn, or they give him a good rest after the early British Events and bring him up earlier for the late summer. Some of course are lucky enough to have more than one horse, so they can work out their programme accordingly.

As in show jumping, no rider can go abroad and compete without first being invited by the host country, and then permission must be obtained from the British Horse Society. In the case of a team representing Britain, the Combined Training Committee make the selection after asking if certain horses and riders will be available. These teams get together often for a week, sometimes more, for extra training and practice before making the trip abroad. Sometimes, as in the case of South Africa, just the riders are invited abroad (usually because of quarantine difficulties in countries on the African continent where African horse sickness is endemic)

86

and the host country provides the mounts.

Although the sport is increasing in popularity in many countries overseas, including America, there are as yet few full-scale Three-Day Events of international standing.

The Americans have now established an international meeting at Ledyard Farm, Hamilton, Massachusetts in June and others are expected to follow. Britain has firmly supported Ledyard Farm and British teams have included Princess Anne and Capt. Mark Phillips.

The Russians are enthusiastic Eventers and the European championships in 1973 were held at Kiev – over a course which caused much controversy, largely because of the siting of the second fence. It was at this fence that Princess Anne, who was defending her European Championship title, had a heavy fall and had to retire.

The West Germans staged the 1975 European Championships at Luhmuhlen about 20 km (12 miles) from Lüneburg. In Austria the principal Three-Day Event is held at Mölbling, usually in July. One of the most popular Events abroad is that at Kalmthout in Belgium, which is an international Trial. The French hold their principal Three-Day Event at Haras du Pin and the Swiss at Colombier.

A very popular overseas Event, especially with British riders, is that held at Boekelo in Holland near the Dutch–German border. It is held in October, which is in the British season.

Ireland holds a Three-Day Event at Punchestown and has staged both European and World Championships there.

Courses at all these Events naturally vary according to the terrain on which they are built, but for every C.C.I. or C.C.I.O. rated Trials (and all the aforementioned are in that category) there is a definite set of rules and standards laid down by the

F.E.I., and before any Trial may start the fences must be examined and passed by a panel of independent and international judges to see that they conform to the required standards. This still gives the individual organizing bodies much leeway on the siting of the fences and their formation.

(*above*) Princess Anne, riding H.M. The Queen's Goodwill, tackles the last part of the 'Sunken Road' fence at Badminton.

(*below*) Princess Anne and Goodwill well over a brush fence.

(*above*) Marjorie Comerford on The Ghillie, riding for Britain as an individual at the European Championships at Kiev in Russia in 1973, takes the second fence which unseated so many riders. She finished 5th overall.

(*below*) Debbie Johnsey, former Junior European Champion, on Nobeark.

Capt. Mark Phillips riding Columbus, owned by H.M. The Queen, seems a long way from the ground during the Cross-country phase of the Badminton Horse Trials.

SHOW JUMPING
PERSONALITIES

Ansell, Col. Sir Michael, C.B.E., D.S.O., D.L. (b. 1905) G.B. President and chairman of the British Equestrian Federation. Was chairman of the British Show Jumping Association from 1944 till 1964, when he was appointed president until 1966. In 1970 he was re-appointed chairman. He held a similar position with the British Horse Society. He became chairman of the British Equestrian Federation on its foundation in 1972. In 1975 he retired as director of both the Royal International and the Horse of the Year Shows at Wembley. Before the Second World War he was in British show jumping teams, and was in the first team ever to go to America from Britain. During the war, while serving with the 5th Royal Inniskilling Dragoon Guards he received wounds which were to leave him in total blindness, and became a prisoner of war. It was during this time that he made plans for the resuscitation of show jumping as a sport in Britain – plans which came to such brilliant fruition, with the establishment of the two great London shows. He was one of the first people to recognize what a 'ready-made' subject show jumping was for the small television screen, and did much to promote it, helping to make show jumping one of Britain's major spectator sports. He is a former High Sheriff of Devonshire, where his home is, near Bideford. Apart from horses and show jumping, his other main interests are fishing and gardening. At one time he grew flowers in Devon on a commercial basis. For many years he was a member of the Bureau of the F.E.I. and when he retired from this office he was made a Member of Honour, a rare distinction. His was the guiding hand in establishing the National Equestrian Centre at Stoneleigh. He was awarded the C.B.E. in 1951 and knighted in 1968 for his services to show jumping.

Arrambide, Dr Hugo (b. 1930) ARGENTINA A member of the Argentine team which came to Britain for the Men's World Show Jumping Championship at Hickstead and the Royal International Show in 1974. In 1964 he was placed 17th overall in the Olympic Games in Tokyo and in 1966 was 3rd in the European Championships at Lucerne. In 1965 won the Rome Grand Prix and tied for the Grand Prix at Aachen the same year with Capt. Piero d'Inzeo, on both occasions riding Chimbote. In 1969 he won the Grand Prix in New York on Adagio.

Backhouse, Mrs Ann (b. 1940) G.B. Daughter of a veterinary surgeon who had a world-wide reputation for performing the operation to help horses' breathing, known as 'hobdaying'. In 1959 she was European Ladies Champion, riding Bandit IV. This was her first year in senior international classes and she was leading lady rider in Paris, Madrid, Lisbon and Le Zoute. She was on the short list for the 1960 Olympics but her horse was not fit and she lost her chance. In 1966 she was again on the short list with Dunboyne but was not chosen. In 1969 won the Horse and Hound Cup at the Royal International Show on Cardinal and on the same horse in 1973 won the Ladies National Championship. First won this title in 1963 on Dunboyne. Won Philips Electrical Stakes at the Royal International Show in 1973 on Concord. Has two children.

Bacon, Kevin (b. 1932) AUSTRALIA Rode in the Australian Olympic team in Mexico in 1968 on

Chichester, when the team finished 9th. Soon after, became leading rider at the New York International, and in 1969 won three competitions in the international show at Berlin.

Bowey, Malcolm (b. 1954) G.B.   From Morpeth in Northumberland, he first jumped abroad as a member of an official British team in 1974 at Olsztyn in Poland where the team was 2nd in the Nations Cup. First came to prominence in 1972 when, riding Partington, he was runner-up for the Victor Ludorum at the Dunhill International Show at Olympia, beaten only by Hartwig Steenken on Simona who went on to become World Champion in 1974. He was then the youngest competitor in the show. In 1974 won a major competition at the Royal Lancashire Show.

Bradley, Caroline (b. 1946) G.B.   Runner-up to Ann Moore for the Ladies European Championship in 1973 and tied for 3rd place in the Ladies World Championship in 1974. Has represented Great Britain at many international shows. Her best-known mount was Franco which she took over for the late Robert Hanson in 1967 and which she rode in winning Nations Cup teams in Poland and Leipzig, contributing to the British win of the President's Cup that year. In 1968 she won the National Championship in Toronto and in 1970 won the British Ladies Championship at the Royal Windsor Show. Both these wins were on Franco. In 1973 on True Lass she was runner-up for the Ladies European Championship, and in 1974 on New Yorker she won the puissance competition at the Horse of the Year Show.

Broome, David, O.B.E. (b. 1940) G.B.   Probably one of the greatest horsemen of this century, certainly with the longest continuous record of top international success. Has twice won an Individual

Olympic Bronze Medal: in Rome on Sunsalve in 1960, and in Mexico on Mister Softee in 1968 Was World Champion in 1970 on Beethoven. Three times European Champion: on Sunsalve in 1961, on Mister Softee in 1967, and again on Mister Softee in 1969. Has won the King George V Gold Cup three times: on Sunsalve in 1960, on Mister Softee in 1966, and on Sportsman in 1972. In 1966 won the Wills British Jumping Derby on Mister Softee. Was 5th in the Men's World Championship at Hickstead in 1974 on Sportsman while defending his World Championship title. Often he has been in the position of not having a really top-class horse to match his ability, but he has soldiered on with lesser animals as in 1959, 1961 and 1962 when he headed the list of money winners for Great Britain. In 1964 was selected for the Olympics at Tokyo and borrowed his brother-in-law's (Ted Edgar's) horse, Jacopo. In his first year as a professional in 1973 he rode for the Esso Petroleum Company, but due to the 1974 oil crisis the contract was not renewed. In 1975 he was sponsored by Harris Carpets. Won the Professionals' Championship at Cardiff with a £2,500 prize from Benson and Hedges in August 1974. In 1970 he received the O.B.E. for his services to show jumping. He is a nationally elected member of the executive committee of the B.S.J.A.

Brown, William ('Buddy') (b. 1956) U.S.A. Was the youngest member of the U.S. team which came to Europe in 1974 and one of the most successful. At the Royal International Show he was 2nd to David Broome in one major competition on a horse called A Little Bit, a former racehorse which had never before competed in international classes, and later the same week won the Calor Gas Under 23 International Championship with the same horse.

Bunn, Douglas (b. 1928) G.B. Although primarily associated in the minds of show jumping enthusiasts with the creation of the All England Show Jumping Course at Hickstead which he started in 1960, and which did more than anything to help promote the success of British riders abroad by giving them a continental type course for the first time in this country, he also had a successful show jumping career. He was in a number of winning Nations Cup teams from 1959–1967, was runner-up for the King George V Gold Cup in 1965, beaten only by the great Hans Winkler of Germany, and won the Grand Prix in Toronto in 1965 on Beethoven. Was called to the bar when he came down from Cambridge, but jumped with the British team abroad whenever he could relinquish his legal duties. For a year, in 1969, he was chairman of the British Show Jumping Association. His ambition is for the Royal International Horse Show to be moved from London and staged at Hickstead, and the future may well see this ambition realized. So far his greatest feat of showmanship and organization was the staging of the Men's World Championship at Hickstead in 1974 when there was a record entry of no less than 16 nations, and a crowd of 30,000 to see the finals.

Chapot, Frank (b. 1934) U.S.A. Was in the U.S. team which came to Europe for the World Championship at Hickstead in 1974 and was one of the two nominated riders for America to contest the title. Riding Main Spring, he was in the last four, when each rider has to compete on the others' horses, and finished finally in 4th place. The next week, at the Royal International Horse Show at Wembley, he won the King George V Cup, the first time it had been won by an American for a decade. He first joined the U.S. Olympic team in 1956 and has been a member of it ever since. In 1965 he married Mary Mairs from California, who was already a well-known show jumping figure.

Coakes, Marion, *see* **Mould,** Marion

Coleman, Ann (b. 1955) G.B. Daughter of television sports commentator, David Coleman. When only 16 won the Ladies National Championship on Havana Royal, the youngest rider ever to do so. In 1972 she was invited to compete in Puerto Rico in an invitation world-wide championship meeting and was placed 2nd. Was often in junior international teams, and in 1974 first competed in a senior team abroad, in the Nations Cup Competition at Olsztyn in Poland, with her horses, Bannerman and Greenside.

Conolly-Carew, The Hon. Diana (b. 1940) EIRE One of Ireland's leading figures in the equestrian field and often *chef d'équipe* to their teams competing overseas, especially their junior teams. In 1966 she won the Dublin Grand Prix on Barrymore, the only pair to go clear, and in 1967 beat Raimondo d'Inzeo and his Olympic horse, Bellevue, in Rome. She has also been runner-up for the Queen Elizabeth Cup and the British Jumping Derby. She is the daughter of Lord and Lady Carew from County Kildare.

Cottle, John (b. 1951) NEW ZEALAND The champion of New Zealand, he made a tour of Europe in 1974 to assess form and the chances for a New Zealand team going to the Olympic Games of 1976. During that time he won many important competitions with his two horses, Rifleman and Warlock.

Davenport, Jean (b. 1944) G.B. Married to former jockey, now trainer, Stephen Davenport, and lives at Mobberly in Cheshire. Won the Queen Elizabeth II Cup in 1974 on All Trumps (which she had ridden in the finals three times on previous occasions) and she won it again in 1975 riding

Hang On. Was in the British team which went to Dinard in 1974. Before her marriage, as Jean Goodwin, she was Ladies National Champion with Hobo in 1967 and also won the Puissance (Moss Bros) Cup at the White City in 1966. Was in the British team at Olsztyn in 1975.

Dawes, Alison (b. 1944) G.B. One of the few riders ever to win the British Jumping Derby twice, which she did on The Maverick VII in 1968, and again in 1973 when the horse's name had been changed to Mr Banbury (Alison had turned professional and was sponsored by the Banbury Building Company). She bought the horse from Douglas Bunn in 1963 when it had a reputation for being difficult. In 1973 she tied for 1st place with Ann Moore in the Queen Elizabeth II Cup. In 1971 she had been runner-up to Ann Moore for the Ladies European Championship. She went to the Olympic Games in Mexico in 1968 as the reserve rider. Was Ladies National Champion in 1969 and 1972, each time with The Maverick.

d'Inzeo, Col. Piero (b. 1923) ITALY Elder of the two famous Italian show jumping brothers. Won an Individual Bronze and a Team Silver Medal at the Olympic Games at Stockholm in 1956 riding Uruguay. Was European Men's Champion in 1959 also riding Uruguay. At the Rome Olympics in 1960 on The Rock won an Individual Silver and a Team Bronze Medal; and in 1964 on Sunbeam won a Team Bronze Medal at the Olympic Games in Tokyo. He has won the King George V Gold Cup three times: in 1957 on Uruguay, in 1961 and 1962 with The Rock; and in 1973 he won the Grand Prix in Rome on his Olympic horse, Easter Light, and won three other competitions at the show.

d'Inzeo, Capt. Raimondo (b. 1925) ITALY

Younger brother of Piero d'Inzeo and a member of the Carabinieri (the mounted police) of Italy. Like his brother he has a fine Olympic record, winning a Team and an Individual Silver Medal at Stockholm in 1956 riding Merano; the Individual Gold Medal in Rome in 1960 and a Team Bronze on Posillipo. He has twice been World Champion, in 1956 and in 1960, the first time on Merano and the second on Gowran Girl; he was 2nd in 1955 and 3rd in 1966. He was one of Italy's two nominees for the Men's World Championship at Hickstead in 1974 when he brought over his No. 1 horse, Bellevue, Irish bred and on which he has scored a number of international successes. Later in 1974 he was Leading Rider of the Show at Dublin.

Edgar, Ted and Elizabeth (b. 1933; b. 1943) G.B. Son of a Warwickshire farmer, Ted is one of the most ebullient characters in show jumping, and he and his wife, who is David Broome's sister, are without doubt the most successful husband-and-wife partnership in show jumping. They ride a string of horses sponsored by the Everest Double Glazing Company, all of which bear the prefix 'Everest' to their names. They also run a stud known as the Everest Stud to breed show horses. Earlier in his career, in 1969, Ted won the King George V Gold Cup on a former American rodeo horse called Uncle Max and the Leading Show Jumper of the Year event at Wembley later the same year, also on Uncle Max. Elizabeth won the first two W. D. and H. O. Wills Young Riders' Championship events at Hickstead in 1960 and 1961 when she was still Elizabeth Broome. She was Ladies National Champion in 1964 and won the title again in 1975.

Fahey, John (b. 1943) AUSTRALIA In the Tokyo Olympics in 1964 he lost the Individual Bronze Medal to Britain's Peter Robeson only after a jump-off, on Bonvale. He rode the same horse in the next Olympics, at Mexico, for the Australian team, and did better than any of his compatriots. In 1972 with Warwick III and The Red Baron he had a successful tour of the British shows, and in 1973 sold Warwick III to Tony Newbery from Devonshire.

Fernyhough, Rowland (b. 1955) G.B.   A native of Montgomeryshire in Wales, he first represented Britain in 1971 as a member of the British junior show jumping team for the European Championships held that year at Hickstead. He rode a horse called Guinea Pig. By 1973 was competing against the 'big boys' and beating them. He won a major international class at Hickstead on Three Castles and in 1974 had his best win to date at the Royal International when he won the Equizole Stakes against fifty-three rivals from more than a dozen nations, again on Three Castles. He had previously won two speed events with this horse at Lucerne.

Fletcher, Graham (b. 1951) G.B. Son of a Yorkshire farmer, he has been show jumping most of his life, graduating from junior to top-flight international status. In 1970 made his first big impact on the south when he won the Cortina Crown (which included the car) for the most points gained at the Horse of the Year Show. His best horse is Buttevant Boy, and in 1971 he rode him as a member of the British team at Aachen, Fontaine-bleau, and Rome. At Dublin, also in 1971, he won the Grand Prix. Was short-listed for the Olympic Games at Munich and won one of the Olympic trials at the British Timken Show, but was not finally selected. In 1974 at the Royal International Show he was 4th in the King George V Cup on Buttevant Boy. The previous week he had been runner-up in the British Jumping Derby. Was also in the British team at the Royal International which won the Nations Cup against six opposing nations, and in which Buttevant Boy jumped two clear rounds.

Fraser, Lady Aileen (b. 1948) G.B.   Well known as Aileen Ross before her marriage, her biggest individual win was in 1972 at Hickstead when she won the National Championship riding Trevarrion. She was in the winning British team for the Nations Cup at Rotterdam in 1969, also riding Trevarrion (owned by Sir Hugh Fraser whom she later married). In 1974 she was in the official British team at La Baule.

Goodwin, Jean, *see* **Davenport,** Jean

Grubb, Tim (b. 1953) G.B.   Comes from Melton Mowbray and rode under National Hunt rules before he took up serious show jumping. First came into the international field in 1974 as a member of the British team which went to Poland. Apart from helping the team come 2nd in the Nations Cup, he was the only member to win two individual classes. Later in 1974 was among the winners in several classes at the Royal International Horse Show competing against some of the world's best riders.

Hobbs, George (b. 1924) G.B.   Has been riding for Britain at home and abroad for more than fifteen years, although the fact that he once held a professional steeplechase jockey's licence meant that he was never eligible to be considered for the Olympic Games. Has three times been runner-up for the King George V Gold Cup and in 1965 won the Victor Ludorum at the Horse of the Year Show on Royal Lord. He farms in Sussex, and has always been one of the staunchest supporters of Hickstead right from the early days. He is chairman of the Rules Committee of the British Show Jumping

Association and a nationally elected member of the executive committee of the B.S.J.A.

Howe, Raymond (b. 1944) G.B. Comes from Biggin Hill in Kent and first started his international career in 1970 when he made his début by being runner-up for the Swiss Grand Prix by a very small margin. Since then he has represented Britain successfully on many occasions and captained the 1974 team which went to Poland.

Jenkins, Rodney (b. 1945) U.S.A. One of the leading professionals in America in the early 1970s; came to Britain in 1974 as a member of the American team competing for the Men's World Championship. He soon became easily identifiable to the crowds by his flaming red hair. Although in the Men's World Championship he did not quite fulfil the promise he had brought with him across the Atlantic, he found his form the following week at the Royal International Horse Show where he won the Grand Prix of Great Britain for the John Player Trophy on Number One Spy and the following week was runner-up to David Broome for the Professionals' Championship at Cardiff Castle. In America he sometimes takes as many as thirty horses to shows with him in his string.

Johnsey, Debbie (b. 1957) G.B. Became Junior European Champion in 1973, but was sometimes in adult classes, often against top-class internationals, in 1972. It was in that year that she first hit the headlines at the Horse of the Year Show when she was runner-up to the then reigning European Ladies Champion, Ann Moore, for the Leading Show Jumper of the Year competition, and again runner-up at the Wills British Championship at Hickstead. On both occasions she was riding Speculator. In 1973 she won the Whitbread Young Riders

Championship at Wembley on Speculator. She is the oldest of four children and lives with her family near the Broomes, close to Chepstow. She has an equally talented young sister, Clair, born in 1963, who before she was 12 had made her mark among junior show jumpers. Debbie was first selected for the British junior team when she was 11, but the rules[1] did not allow her to compete, even in junior international teams, because she was too young. She is coached by her father who rode as an amateur steeplechase jockey.

Kellett, Iris (b. 1926) EIRE Was the first winner of the Queen Elizabeth II Cup in 1949 when it was known as the Princess Elizabeth Cup. She also won it again in 1951. In 1969 she won the Ladies European Championship on Morning Light, the year the competition was held in her native Dublin. After that she retired from international show jumping, selling Morning Light for £30,000 to Frenchman Hubert Parot. Miss Kellett runs a most successful string of horses; her principal rider (until 1975) was her brilliant pupil, Eddie Macken, who, at 23, was runner-up for the Men's World Championship in 1974 on the former hunter, Pele.

Kerr, Barbara (b. 1947) CANADA Competed for Canada in the Ladies World Championship in France in 1974 and won the first leg but was beaten overall by Janou Tissot of France. As Barbara Simpson (before her marriage) she was Leading Lady Rider of Canada. In 1971 was in winning Nations Cup teams for Canada in New York and Toronto. Also in that year was a member of the Canadian team which won the Gold Medal in the Pan-American Games held at Cali in Columbia.

[1] A person may compete in a junior (international) team from the beginning of the year of their 14th birthday until the end of the year of their 18th.

Kusner, Kathy (b. 1940) U.S.A. Became a member of the U.S. equestrian team in 1962, winning the U.S. President's Cup in that year. She rode for the U.S.A. in the Olympics at Tokyo and Munich and in 1965 was runner-up to Marion Mould for the Ladies World Championship. Won the Irish Grand Prix in 1964 and 1965 riding the same horse, Untouchable, both times and was the first rider to win twice in succession. In 1967 won the Ladies European Championship, also on Untouchable. Her first love, however, is really racing, and she became the first woman in the U.S.A. to hold a jockey's licence.

Lefebvre, Janou, *see* **Tissot,** Janou

Ligges, Fritz W. GERMANY Started as a Three-Day Event rider and won the Individual Bronze Medal in the Tokyo Olympics before turning to show jumping. Was a member of the Olympic Gold Medal-winning German team in the Munich Olympics in 1972.

Llewellyn, Lt-Col. Harry, C.B.E., O.B.E. (b. 1911) G.B. Although he has won many international triumphs with numerous horses, he will always be remembered among the great names of show jumping for his feats with Foxhunter. They were members of the British team which won the Olympic Gold Medal for show jumping at Helsinki in 1952, the only time Britain has ever won a gold for this branch of equestrianism. They three times won the King George V Gold Cup, in 1948, 1950 and 1953. Altogether he won more than 150 international competitions before he retired from show jumping. The famous Foxhunter novice jumping competitions were his idea, first taken up by the London *Evening Standard* and later by the *Daily Express* and named after his beloved horse.

He is one of the British Horse Society representatives at F.E.I. meetings. From 1967–1969 he was chairman of the British Show Jumping Association, and in 1974 was elected president. His first great love was steeplechasing and in 1936 he was 2nd in the Grand National on Ego, beaten only by the great Reynoldstown. In 1937, again on Ego, he was 4th. He was awarded the O.B.E. in 1944 and became a C.B.E. in 1953.

Macken, Eddie (b. 1950) EIRE   First made his mark in the Irish junior teams. In 1972 on Oatfield Hills tied for 1st place with Graham Fletcher for the Calor Gas International Under 23 Championship at the Horse of the Year Show, and in 1973 won the Moss Bros Championship for puissance at the Royal International Horse Show, also on Oatfield Hills. His best performance to date, however, was in the Men's World Championship in 1974 when he was runner-up for the title, having won two of the three legs on the way to the final on Miss Iris Kellett's Pele. In 1975 he decided to leave Ireland and join Paul Schockemohle's stable in W. Germany. He won the Victor Ludorum at the 1975 Royal International Horse Show riding Boomerang.

Mairs, Mary (b. 1944) U.S.A.   Was only 18 when she first joined the U.S. equestrian team. In 1963 at Sao Paolo she made history in the Pan-American Games by being the first American and the first woman to win an Individual Gold Medal (riding Tomboy). In 1964, at the Royal International Horse Show, she won the John Player Trophy, the Saddle of Honour and the Lorriners' Cup. In 1968 she won the Queen Elizabeth II Cup riding White Lightning. Has nine times been in the U.S. Nations Cup team and represented the United States in the 1964 (Tokyo) and the 1968 (Mexico) Olympic Games. She married U.S. Olympic rider Frank

Chapot in 1965 and they have a daughter.

Matz, Michael (b. 1953) U.S.A. Became a member of the American team in 1973 and came to Europe with them in 1974. In 1972 won the North American Championship at Detroit and the Cleveland Grand Prix. Lives in Ohio.

McEvoy, Michele (b. 1953) U.S.A. Came to Europe with the U.S. team in 1974. Was 3rd in the Rome Grand Prix. Lives in Summit, New Jersey.

McMahon, Paddy (b. 1933) G.B. In spite of his Irish-sounding name, he was born in Derby. First rose to international fame in 1971 when he joined Fred Hartill at Wolverhampton to ride Pennwood Forge Mill, one of the outstandingly successful horses of the '70s. First went abroad for Britain with this horse in 1971 and won the Grand Prix at Ostend. Won the Victor Ludorum at the Horse of the Year Show and the Courvoisier Supreme Championship, 1972. In 1973 the pair won the Men's European Championship at Hickstead and the next week went on to win the Horse and Hound Cup and the King George V Gold Cup at the Royal International Horse Show. He was on the short list for the 1972 Olympics but was not selected. With David Broome was chosen to ride for Britain in the Men's World Championship in 1974, but after a good beginning up among the leaders he tailed off so disappointingly that Mr Hartill had the horse X-rayed and it was discovered that he had a badly pulled neck muscle.

Moore, Ann (b. 1950) G.B. Her home is at Knowle in Warwickshire. In 1968 won the Junior European Championship title, having been in the British junior team for three years before that. First joined the senior international team in Spain in 1970. In 1971 won the Ladies European

Championship in Switzerland on her thoroughbred, Psalm, and retained the title in France in 1973. Was a member of the British team at the Olympics in Munich in 1972 and won an Individual Silver Medal, again on Psalm. In 1974 she seemed all set to win the Ladies World title, but Psalm developed leg trouble and that ended his show jumping career. Ann announced her retirement from competitive sport to concentrate on breeding horses. In autumn 1974 she began a new career as a television commentator.

Mould, Marion (b. 1947) G.B. With her little horse, Stroller, as Marion Coakes (she married National Hunt jockey, David Mould, in 1969) she became an almost legendary figure in the 1960s. When only 18 she won the Ladies World Championship with Stroller at Hickstead in 1965. That same year she became the youngest competitor ever to win the Queen Elizabeth II Cup (a record still standing) and Stroller – 14.2 h.h (144 cm) – was the smallest horse ever to do so. (They won again in 1971.) In 1968 they won the Individual Silver Medal at the Olympic Games in Mexico, Marion being the first woman ever to do so. The same year they were equal 3rd in the Ladies European Championship. The previous year the fantastic little horse won the Wills British Jumping Derby at Hickstead, one of the toughest courses in the show jumping world. Always specialists of the international ring at Hickstead, they set up a record of winning the Wills Hickstead Gold Medal (for points gained in major events during the year) for five years in succession, from 1965 to 1970. Stroller officially retired in 1973. For a time Marion stepped out of the international limelight and concentrated on bringing on two young horses, Dunlynne and John Gamble. She returned to the international field in 1974 when she stepped into the breach at the last moment for the Ladies World Championship after Ann Moore announced her retirement. She started well, but an unlucky fall eventually put her out of the running.

Newbery, Tony (b. 1954) G.B. Comes from Devon and started riding show ponies when a very young child. It was not until 1973, however, that he came to international fame when he acquired Warwick III, the former Australian Olympic horse which used to be ridden by John Fahey. After some home successes he was selected to go with the British team to Aachen, one of the top-ranking international shows in the world. Was in the British team which came 2nd in the Nations Cup, beaten only by the 1972 Olympic Gold Medal-winning German team, and was individually runner-up in the Grand Prix. In the winter of 1973 he was invited to join David Broome and Harvey Smith in a tour of North America and Canada. Riding Warwick III, he won once, had two seconds and six thirds, and was placed in several other competitions competing against the best riders of America, Canada and Germany. In 1974, again on Warwick III, he was runner-up for the King George V Cup, and on another horse, Snaffles, was 3rd in the Moss Bros Cup for puissance at the Royal International Horse Show at Wembley. Was in the official British team for the Dublin Horse Show in 1974.

Oliver, Alan (b. 1932) G.B. Started competitive riding on his father's horses when he was only 11, and although has jumped abroad for British teams, his major successes have been on the home front. First joined the official British team in 1951 with Red Admiral on whom he won the National Championship jointly, tying with another of his mounts, Red Knight. Was short-listed for the 1952 and the 1956 Olympics but was not selected either time. Won the National Championship again in 1959 with John Gilpin. In 1953 on Galway Bay tied for 1st place in the Lonsdale Puissance at the Royal International Horse Show (then at the White City) with Col. Harry Llewellyn and Piero d'Inzeo. In the early 1960s he had a hard time finding horses to replace his formidable string of the '50s but eventually was back in the forefront with Sweep and Pitz Palu. 1969 was his best year, when he won two competitions in Rome, was in the Nations Cup-winning team in Barcelona (one of the only two British victories that year), won the National Championship again, and altogether won sixty-nine major competitions during the season, including the Ronson Trophy Victor Ludorum (for the second time) at the Horse of the Year Show. His wife is Alison Oliver, the Event specialist who is Princess Anne's coach and trainer. He is a nationally elected member of the executive committee of the B.S.J.A.

Pessoa, Nelson (b. 1935) BRAZIL Now lives in France but still competes under the Brazilian flag. Became professional in 1974. Won the Men's European Championship in 1966 and has won the British Jumping Derby once and the Hamburg Derby three times.

Pritchard, Ken (b. 1944) G.B. Was selected as an official member of the British team for the 1974 Dublin Horse Show with Longboot and Torchlight. Comes from Rugeley in Staffordshire. Made his mark as a fast rider on Longboot at the Royal International Horse Show at Wembley in 1974 and won the opening competition at Cardiff Castle at the Benson and Hedges Show the following week. Competed for Britain in Holland, 1974.

Pyrah, Malcolm (b. 1941) G.B. Comes from Yorkshire. Was on the short list for the Men's World Championship in 1974 but was not selected. He was, however, chosen for the official team for the Royal International Horse Show at Wembley that year and was in the winning Nations Cup team, jumping two clear rounds on the mare Trevarrion. Earlier in the year, riding Law Court, he had been Britain's only winner at the Rome International Show. In October 1974 at Wembley won the Courvoisier Cognac Supreme Championship on the former Australian Olympic mare, April Love – a contest which carried the record prize money for 1st place of £3,000.

Ridland, Robert (b. 1951) U.S.A. Was the reserve rider for the U.S. team for the 1972 Olympics and has competed in Europe in 1970, 1971, 1972 and 1974. Was in the U.S. Nations Cup team which came 2nd at the Royal International Horse Show at Wembley in 1974.

Robeson, Peter (b. 1929) G.B. The veteran member of the British international squad, first joining the team in 1947 on a mare called Craven A. In 1956 was in the British team at the Stockholm Olympics where Britain won a Team Bronze Medal. In 1964 was again in the British Olympic team, riding his own Firecrest, and won an Individual Bronze Medal in Tokyo. In 1967 he won the King George V Cup with Firecrest. Altogether he has been included in an international team more than eighty times. In 1974 he won the Everest Double Glazing Championship on Grebe.

Ross, Aileen, *see* **Fraser,** Lady Aileen

Saywell, Michael (b. 1942) G.B. A farmer's son from Lincolnshire, he first got a foot on the international ladder when he went to Trevor Banks' stables in Yorkshire. Here he rode Hideaway, a half Clydesdale which was bought for £80, and made his first international début on the horse at La Baule in 1970, where he won the Grand Prix. In 1971 became a regular member of British teams abroad and in 1972 was short-listed for the Olympic Games in Munich. He went very well in all the Olympic trials; at the Great Yorkshire Show he had the only clear round, and in the final trial, the Wills Grand Prix at Hickstead, he was 2nd. He and Hideaway were selected for the team which went to Munich, and had the best record of the four members. Shortly after Munich he left Trevor Banks' stable and returned to his native Lincolnshire where he rode for John Taylor. Later he returned to the Trevor Banks/Harvey Smith stable.

Schockemohle, Alwin (b. 1937) W. GERMANY When he was 17 became a pupil of the great German horseman, Hans Winkler, at the German Equestrian Federation's school at Warendorf. Was the reserve rider for the German team at the 1956 Olympics and in 1957 achieved his first international win at Aachen. Was in the Gold Medal-winning team at the Rome Olympics in 1960. Has five times been in the first three for the European Championship but has never yet won the title. At the Mexico Olympics in 1968 was in the German team which won the Bronze Medal and had the best score of the competition. On Donald Rex, he won the Grand Prix at Aachen the same year. Was 2nd in the British Jumping Derby in 1970 after a jump-off where he unfortunately injured his back in a fall and was out of action until 1971. In 1972 won the Irish Grand Prix on The Robber. In 1974 was a member of the German team which competed at the Royal International Horse Show. In 1975 he won the King George V Gold Cup and the John Player Trophy riding Rex the Robber.

Schockemohle, Paul (b. 1944) W. GERMANY Younger brother of Alwin, he joined the German team in 1971. Has concentrated on training horses rather than actual show jumping. He had successes in Britain in 1974 at Wembley.

Simon, Hugo AUSTRIA Was able to claim dual nationality for the 1972 Olympic Games in Munich, being a West German but born in Austria. As he was not included in the West German team, he opted for his Austrian nationality, becoming a member of the Austrian team. In 1974 was in the last four for the World Championship at Hickstead on Lavendel and finally finished 3rd overall behind Steenken of Germany and Eddie Macken of Eire.

Simpson, Barbara, *see* **Kerr,** Barbara

Smith, Harvey (b. 1938) G.B. As a boy competed in junior classes at small local shows but first came to the public eye in 1954 when he bought a horse called Farmer's Boy for less than £50 at a sale in his native Yorkshire. Four years later he was riding the horse with the British team at Dublin. In 1968 was a member of the British team at the Mexico Olympics riding Madison Time and again at Munich in 1972 with Summertime. Shortly after he became the first British rider to turn professional. In 1973 and 1974 his horse Salvador was in the top ten money-winning horses of Britain. Has won almost every major competition in Britain on one or other of his ever-changing string of horses, including the King George V Gold Cup, the British Jumping Derby (three times), and the British Grand Prix for the John Player Trophy, no less than five times. In 1972 he went into partnership with Trevor Banks, a fellow Yorkshireman with an eye for a horse at a bargain. Harvey became a household name not so much for his prowess in the

Frank Chapot, one of the top American show jumpers, on Main Spring at Hickstead during the World Championships in 1974.

Germany's ace rider, Alwin Schockemohle, with one of his best horses, Rex the Robber. He is a regular competitor in Britain and is seen here jumping at Hickstead.

Marion Mould on Stroller, one of the great horse personalities of all time. He carried Marion from junior classes (his size was officially in the pony category) to an Olympic Silver Medal. He had an official retiring ceremony at Hickstead in 1973. (*far below*) David Broome on the American-bred Philco on which he won the Servis Silver Spurs plus £1,000 cash at the Horse of the Year Show in 1975 for the highest-placed horse in the show.

Eddie Macken, the Irishman who joined the Schockemohle stable in Germany in 1975, riding Pele, the horse on which he was runner-up for the World Championship in 1974.

show jumping arena as for an incident at Hickstead in 1971 when he made a V-sign gesture (V for victory, Harvey insisted) in front of the judges' box after winning the £2,000 prize for the British Jumping Derby, and was disqualified. Later, an enquiry by the B.S.J.A. stewards exonerated him.

Smythe, Pat, O.B.E. (b. 1928) G.B. One of the world's leading show jumping personalities for many years. Now Mrs Koechlin-Smythe, she makes her home in Switzerland, though frequently visits Britain where she often keeps young stock. It was Pat who helped to make the public show jumping conscious in the years immediately following the Second World War when, with her famous horses Prince Hal and Tosca, and later with Mr Robert Hanson's Flanagan (which he eventually gave to her), she won competitions all over the world. She was the first woman to compete in show jumping in the Olympic Games when, in 1956, she was a member of the British team which won the Bronze Medal at Stockholm, and was also in the British team which competed in Rome in 1960. She is the only woman to have won the Ladies European Championship four times, in 1957, 1961, 1962 and 1963, each time riding Flanagan. In 1958 won the Queen Elizabeth II Cup on Mr Pollard. In 1956 she was awarded the O.B.E. She often acts as *chef d'équipe* to British teams on the Continent especially in Switzerland. Since she has given up competitive riding she has made a second career of writing and has published a large number of successful books.

Steenken, Hartwig (b. 1941) W. GERMANY Riding Simona, a chestnut Hanoverian mare foaled in 1958, he won the Men's World Championship title in 1974 at Hickstead. Was in the German team for the 1972 Munich Olympics when they won the

Gold Medal, again riding Simona. In 1971 became European Men's Champion at Aachen, with Britain's Harvey Smith close behind him. In 1973 he was out of action for the season when he broke his leg twice, and so was prevented from defending his European title.

Steinkraus, William ('Bill') (b. 1925) U.S.A. Won the Individual Gold Medal at the 1968 Mexico Olympics on Snowbound. This was the fifth time he had been in the U.S. team for the Olympics. In 1952 at Helsinki he was a member of the team that won a Bronze Medal and in 1960 helped them win the Team Silver Medal in Rome and again in 1972 in Munich. Has twice won the King George V Gold Cup, in 1956 on First Boy and in 1964 on Sinjon. Does not now take such an active part in the international field, preferring to spend more time at home. He is a keen and talented amateur musician.

Tagle, Roberto (b. 1946) ARGENTINA Came over to Britain with the Argentine team in 1974 and although did not compete for the World Championship, he won the Wills International Grand Prix on Simple, having previously won a major class at a 'warm up' at the Kent County Show. Was one of six equal firsts in a section of the Horse and Hound Cup at the 1974 Royal International Show, again riding Simple.

Tissot, Janou (b. 1945) FRANCE Was in the French Silver Medal-winning team at the Olympic Games in Tokyo in 1964 when she was only 19. In 1974 became the Ladies World Champion at La Baule, the last time the World Championship was held in separate sections for men and women. She was born Janou Lefebvre; her mother was Chinese and her father French, working in Indo-China.

Her husband is a member of the watch-making family.

Westwood, Alison, *see* **Dawes,** Alison

Winkler, Hans (b. 1926) W. GERMANY Won the Individual Gold Medal at the 1956 Stockholm Olympic Games riding Halla and helped the Germans win the Team Gold; in 1960 again won a Team Gold with Halla at Rome, and also in 1964 in Tokyo riding Fidelitas. In 1968 helped the German team win a Bronze Medal in the Mexico Olympics. Twice won the Men's World Championship and once the European. Has twice won the King George V Gold Cup, and in 1972 again helped the German team win the Gold Medal at the Munich Olympics, riding Torphy. He has been a member of the German Nations Cup team in more than seventy competitions in all parts of the world. He is captain of the German team and a chief instructor at the headquarters of Germany's Equestrian Federation at Warendorf.

Wouters, Harry HOLLAND A member of the Dutch team which came to Britain in 1974 for the Men's World Championship. At the Royal International Horse Show he won the Horse and Hound Cup, the first major prize of the week, and the first Dutchman ever to do so. In the Nations Cup he was a member of his country's team which came 3rd, beating the much-fancied Germans whom many had tipped to win.

HORSE TRIALS
PERSONALITIES

Allhusen, Major Derek (b. 1914) G.B. Captained the British Olympic team in Mexico in 1968 when Britain won the Team Gold Medal, and he won the Individual Silver Medal on Lochinvar although then aged 54. In 1957, 1967 and 1969 was in the team which won the European Championship for Britain. Served in the 9th Lancers during and before the Second World War. He also breeds horses, notably Laurieston, the horse on which Richard Meade won the Individual Gold Medal at the Munich Olympics in 1972. Does not now take a competitive part in the big Trials.

Anne, H.R.H. The Princess (b. 1950) G.B. Princess Anne rode with marked success in Pony Club Trials for some years before she left school. While still at Benenden School she first appeared in competition in public when she was a member of the Battle Riding Club quadrille team which qualified for the Horse of the Year Show at Wembley in 1968 and was finally placed 2nd. When she left school she was determined to embark on an equestrian career and made a good start by winning the Horse Trials at Windsor in 1969 on Royal Ocean, followed the same year by a win at Osberton with Doublet. Doublet was bred by H.M. The Queen and originally intended as a polo pony, but he grew too big and was taken over by Princess Anne. In 1971 she made her international début with him at the Badminton Horse Trials and finished a credit-able 5th. She was short-listed for the European Championships to be held later that year at Burghley. Finally, the selectors decided not to put the strain of being a team member on her, but that she should compete as an individual. She won the Individual Championship, beating the top riders from many countries. In 1972 she was short-listed for the Olympic Games on Doublet when the bad luck which was to plague the horse for the rest of his life, and end in his death in 1974, struck. He developed leg trouble and had to be withdrawn from all competitions for a year. In 1973 she took Goodwill (a horse which had started on the international road as a show jumper) to Kiev to defend her European Championship title but he had a fall at the second fence in the Cross-country course and Princess Anne injured her shoulder and withdrew from the Event. In 1974 Princess Anne again competed at Badminton, riding Goodwill; she finished 4th on him and was short-listed for the 1974 World Championships at Burghley. She rode as an individual at Burghley and finished 12th overall from 58 starters. In 1975 was a member of the British Silver Medal-winning team for the European Championships held in Germany. In 1973 she married one of Britain's outstanding riders, Capt. Mark Phillips.

Boylan, Major Eddie (b. 1925) EIRE Was in the Irish team which won the World Championship at Burghley in 1966, and in 1967 won the Individual European Championship at Punchestown, Co. Kildare. Won the Badminton Horse Trials in 1965 on Durlas Eile, a horse subsequently sold to Canada before the Mexico Olympics for a reputed £19,000, a record price at that time for an Event horse.

Bullen, Jane (b. 1948) G.B. Is a State Registered Nurse, having qualified at the Middlesex Hospital, London. The hospital gave her special leave to compete in the Olympic Games in Mexico in 1968 with the British team, which won the Gold Medal. She was the first woman ever to be part of a British team at an Olympic Three-Day Event. (Women were not eligible until 1964.) She won the Badminton Horse Trials in 1968 (having been 5th in 1967) riding Our Nobby, a tiny horse only 15 h.h. (152 cm) which was her mount in Mexico. She was 3rd both years at Burghley.

Collins, Chris (b. 1940) G.B. Former leading amateur National Hunt jockey who took up Horse Trials in 1970 and rapidly made his mark. In 1973 after the Burghley Three-Day Event he bought Smokey VI, a 9-year-old Irish-bred horse by Sadlers Wells, from Bill Powell-Harris, an Irish Three-Day Event rider. In 1974, with Smokey VI, he was a member of the British team for the World Championships, and with another horse, Centurion, he was short-listed to compete as an individual. In 1973 won the Pardubice race in Czechoslovakia, the first Englishman ever to do so. He is head of a perfumery firm. His sister, Anna, is also a Horse Trials rider.

Comerford, Marjorie (b. 1944) G.B. From Spalding in Lincolnshire, Mrs Comerford first came to prominence in Horse Trials in 1971. In 1973 she finished 7th at Badminton and was selected to go to the European Championships held at Kiev in Russia as an individual rider. Riding The Ghillie, a bay gelding sired by Tynwald and owned by Mr C. Harrison of Spalding, she achieved the considerable success of being placed 5th overall. At another foreign Trials in 1973 at Boekelo in Holland she was placed 7th.

Davidson, Bruce (b. 1950) U.S.A. A member of the U.S. team which won the World Championship title held in Britain in 1974 and he himself won the individual title on Irish Cap. Was 3rd at the

Badminton Horse Trials in 1974 and placed 1st and 3rd in the Combined Training and Dressage Championships at the Royal International Horse Show the same summer. He is from Massachusetts.

Gordon-Watson, Mary (b. 1948) G.B. Became individual World Champion on her father's Cornishman V in 1970 at Punchestown and was a member of the British team which won the World Championship. In 1969 at Haras du Pin in France she won the European Championship. In 1972 she rode Cornishman in the Munich Olympic Games with the British team which won the Gold Medal. She lives in Dorset and is a keen point-to-point rider.

Hatherly, Sue (b. 1952) G.B. Has had successes on a number of different horses, but it was the ex-Australian Olympic team horse, Harley, which brought her international fame. In 1973 the pair won the first international Three-Day Event held in America, at Ledyard Farm, Massachusetts, having come 3rd at Burghley. The same year they won the Midland Bank Open Championship at Cirencester and were placed 9th overall at Badminton. An injury early in the season put the horse out of major competitions in 1974, and she lost her chance of being considered for the British team for the World Championships that year. She lives in Kent. The horse is now owned by the British Equestrian Federation.

Hill, Bertie (b. 1927) G.B. Lives in South Molton, Devon, and was a member of the British team in three Olympic Games: in 1952 at Helsinki, in 1956 at Stockholm, when Britain won the Gold Medal, and in 1960 in Rome. Is now trainer to the British team and his son Tony (born 1954) is carrying on the family tradition as a competitor. He was a member of the winning British team in 1972 for the Junior European Championship, riding Maid

Marion. One of Mr Hill's most distinguished pupils is Capt. Mark Phillips, who was in the Olympic Gold Medal-winning team at Munich in 1972, and who rode Maid Marion to victory at the Burghley Horse Trials in 1973 when Tony dropped out because of an injury. Capt. Phillips also rode Mr Hill's Chicago in the successful British team for the 1970 World Championship.

Hodgson, Janet (b. 1948) G.B. This Warwickshire rider has done more than any other to show that although Eventing is a tough sport, it is not, as some think, too tough for women. She was a member of the British team at the European Championships at Kiev in Russia in 1973 when, riding Larkspur, she had two crashing falls, but somehow remounted to keep the team in the competition, and finished with blood streaming from a smashed face and jaw. Even the Russians were impressed with her pluck and gave her a special prize of a gold watch. Thanks to her, Britain took the Bronze Medal. In 1973 she was nominated Equestrian Personality of the Year by the British Equestrian Writers Association. After a severe fall at Badminton in 1971, she went on that same year to win at Chatsworth with Larkspur, and also at Boekelo in Holland. In 1972 she was short-listed for the Olympics but was not finally chosen. A few weeks after the Games, however, she won the Burghley Trials. Other successes include 3rd place in 1968 at Stoneleigh with Larkspur – his first Horse Trial – and in 1970 placed 4th at Burghley and 5th at Rahinston in Ireland. In 1974 she finished 4th in the World Championship at Burghley and was 2nd at Badminton, riding Larkspur on both occasions.

Holgate, Virginia (b. 1955) G.B. A young west country rider from Silverton, near Exeter in Devon, she became Junior European Champion in France in 1973 on Dubonnet, and was a member of the British team which won the team title. In 1972 she had competed as an individual in the junior championships which were then held at Eridge in Kent. In her first major competition among adults, at the Midland Bank Open Championship at Cirencester in 1973, she came 7th overall.

Jones, Staff-Sgt R. S. ('Ben') G.B. Royal Army Veterinary Corps. Was a member of the Olympic Gold Medal-winning British team in Mexico in 1968 when he rode The Poacher belonging to Mr Martin Whiteley, who dropped out because of back trouble. Finished 5th in the individual placings. In 1967, riding Foxdor, and in 1969, riding The Poacher, he was a member of the winning British team in the European Championships. Was 3rd at Badminton in 1968 with Foxdor, on which he had been placed 7th the previous year. Unfortunately Foxdor later died of a heart attack while in training for the Olympics.

Meade, Richard (b. 1938) G.B. One of the world's outstanding Horse Trials riders, and a triple Olympic Gold Medallist. In 1968 at the Olympic Games in Mexico was in the winning British team, and in 1972 in Munich was in the Gold Medal-winning team and also won the Individual Gold Medal on Laurieston. In 1970 was in the British team which won the World Championship, and that year he also won Badminton, on both occasions riding The Poacher. On his horse, Barberry, he was 2nd in the individual placings in the World Championships at Burghley in 1966. Was in the team which finished 3rd in the European Championships at Moscow in 1965 and in Kiev in 1973. He won the Three Day Event at Boekelo in Holland in 1973 on Wayfarer, the horse belonging to Mrs Henry Wilkin which he rode at Kiev. Was a member ot the British team for the 1974 World Championship at Burghley when Britain came 2nd. Wayfarer was retired from Eventing in 1975. When he is not riding he works with a firm of insurance brokers in London. His family home is in Monmouthshire.

Morgan, Laurie (b. 1915) AUSTRALIA First competed in Britain in 1955 when he came 4th individually in the European Championships which that year were held at the invitation of H.M. The Queen in Windsor Great Park. In the 1960 Olympics at Rome he captained the Australian team which won the Gold Medal, and he himself won the Individual Gold Medal on Salad Days. The following year, 1961, he won the Badminton Horse Trials, again on Salad Days, and with his other horse, College Master, won the Foxhunter Steeplechases at Cheltenham and Liverpool. Has now joined the ranks of the judges, and in 1974 at the Royal International Horse Show at Wembley he judged two dressage championships.

Parker, Bridget (b. 1939) G.B. Was a member of the British team which won the Gold Medal at the Munich Olympics in 1972, being called upon to ride only a few hours before the Three-Day Event started (having travelled with her horse, Cornish Gold, as one of the reserve riders). In 1970 she won at Windsor and Crookham and was originally selected as a member of the British team for the World Championships held at Punchestown but in the end did not go. In 1969 she was 2nd at Chatsworth and at Punchestown. In 1974, with Cornish Gold, she was a member of the British team for the World Championships at Burghley and helped win the Team Silver Medal. Her home is in Frome, Somerset.

Phillips, Capt. Mark (b. 1948) G.B. Rode in his first senior Horse Trials in 1967 at Everdon on

Rock On after competing in Pony Club Trials teams for five successive years. Later in 1967 came 4th at Burghley and early in 1968 was again 4th at Badminton. This led to his being selected as reserve rider for the 1968 Olympics in Mexico and he was given special leave from Sandhurst (where he was then a cadet) to train. In 1969 rode as an individual in the European Championships at Haras du Pin in France, and in 1970 rode on Mr Bertie Hill's Chicago in the British team for the World Championships at Punchestown, helping Britain win the title. In 1971, riding Great Ovation, a horse he owned jointly with his aunt, Miss Flavia Phillips, he won Badminton and repeated the win again in 1972 – only the second time the same horse has won for two successive years. He was in the team which won the European Championship for Britain at Burghley in 1971, and in 1972 was a member of the British Gold Medal-winning Olympic team at Munich. He tried for the Badminton hat trick with Great Ovation in 1973, but the horse went lame during the Roads and Tracks phase. In 1974, however, he again won, this time riding the Queen's big grey, Columbus, and is one of the few ever to have won Badminton three times. In 1973 he won the Burghley Three-Day Event on Mr Hill's Maid Marion, and later in the year won the Dutch International Event at Boekelo on Laureate, on which he also won the Open at Wylye and the 'Griffin' section at Tidworth, also in 1973. It was in that year that his marriage to H.R.H. The Princess Anne took place. In 1974 he rode Columbus in the British team for the World Championships at Burghley when Britain came 2nd. Was well in the lead for the individual title when the horse went lame after the second day and he had to withdraw.

Plumb, Michael (b. 1940) U.S.A. Comes from

Maryland. Was a member of the U.S. Olympic Three-Day Event team which won the team Silver Medals in 1964, 1968 and 1972. Was also in the U.S. team which won the Gold Medals in 1963 and 1967 in the Pan-American Games. Five times in seven years he was nominated leading Three-Day Event rider in the United States. Was in the team which won the World Championship at Burghley in 1974 and won the Individual Silver Medal on Good Mixture.

Prior-Palmer, Lucinda (b. 1953) G.B.   A member of the British team at Kiev for the European Championships in 1973 with Be Fair on which she had won the Badminton Event earlier in the year. In 1972 won the Midland Bank Open Championship at Cirencester, having been 5th that year at Badminton and 4th at Burghley, and short-listed for the Olympic team. Just before she graduated out of junior class she was a member of the winning British junior team which won the junior European Championship in Germany in 1971. By 1974 was on the short list for the British team for the World Championships. Eventually rode as an individual and finished 10th overall. In 1975 became European Champion on Be Fair.

Roycroft, James ('Bill') O.B.E. (b. 1915) AUSTRALIA   'Bill' Roycroft, as he is always known, is everyone's conception of the 'tough Aussie'. He has been a member of the Australian Olympic team three times. In Rome in 1960, where they won the Gold Medal, he had a very bad fall from his horse during the Cross-country course. The horse bolted and Bill lay semi-conscious. The horse, called Our Solo, was retrieved, and somehow Bill remounted and finished the course. He was then rushed to hospital by helicopter. Another member of the team, however, was eliminated, which would have meant the Australians having to withdraw since the rules stipulate there must be three riders competing in each phase. So, in spite of all medical protests, Bill left hospital the next day with his injuries strapped up and completed the Show Jumping phase, and Australia took the team Gold Medal (as well as Individual Gold and Silver). That same year, on Our Solo, he won at Badminton. In 1965 he became the first rider at Badminton to enter and to complete the course with three different horses. They were placed 2nd and 6th in the Great Badminton Event and the remaining horse was 2nd in the 'Little Badminton'. (For a few years Badminton was divided into two sections, 'Great' and 'Little', differing in classification, but the idea was dropped after 1965.) Captained the Australian team in the Mexico Olympics where they won the Bronze Medal in 1968, and in 1969 received the O.B.E. for his services to equestrian sport. Has two sons, Wayne and Barry, both of whom have also ridden for Australia.

Sutherland, Lorna (b. 1944) G.B. A native of Aberdeenshire and one of the best-known and most successful women Event riders in the country. In 1971, with Peer Gynt won the 'mini' Olympics held at Munich in a run-through for the Olympic Games in 1972. She was picked as one of the reserves for the team in 1972. She started off as a show jumper, competing in America when she was only 16, but a year later, after a brief spell of show jumping in Britain, she concentrated on Horse Trials. In 1967 she won the Burghley Trials on a skewbald, Popadom, on which she competed as an individual in the World Championships at Punchestown in 1970 and finished 12th. She was unable to compete the following year in the European Championships at Burghley owing to an injury after a fall at the Lockerbie Horse Trials in the previous month.

However 1971 was not without success for her as Peer Gynt won the Rothman's Combined Training Championships at the Royal International Horse Show. In 1970 she became the only woman ever to ride three horses at Badminton, emulating the record of the Australian, Bill Roycroft, and only the second rider ever to do so. She finished in the money with two of them. This feat meant she had ridden in one afternoon a total of 51 miles, spent $4\frac{1}{2}$ hours in the saddle, and negotiated 140 obstacles for the Speed and Endurance phase alone.

Thompson, Virginia (b. 1951) G.B.   Comes from Market Harborough, Leicestershire. Her best-known horse is Cornish Duke on which she came 3rd in the Badminton Horse Trials in 1973 and was short-listed in that year for the European Championships. Was short-listed in 1974 for the World Championships at Burghley where she rode as an individual but did not complete the course. Her first notable win was in 1972 at the Brigstock Trials.

Thorne, Diana (b. 1953) G.B.   Diana Thorne, who lives near Leamington Spa in Warwickshire, is also a keen point-to-point rider, and on one occasion both her sister and herself and their father competed in the same race. Diana started seriously in Horse Trials in 1972 with a horse called The Kingmaker. It was a spectacular start, for they won the novice classes at Batsford and at Meriden, and ended the season by winning the Golden Griffin Trophy for 1st place in the Midland Bank National Novice Championship at Cirencester. In 1973 they were 2nd at Burghley and won two other Events at Kinlet and Corbridge.

Warren-Codrington, Elizabeth Buist (b. 1933) RHODESIA   One of Rhodesia's leading Trials riders who has represented Rhodesia on many occasions since 1963. She rode for her country in the Whitbread Horse Trials at Johannesburg in 1968, 1969 and 1970, being placed each time and winning in 1969. Has also won in Salisbury, in Umtali and in Wankie. She has represented Rhodesia on several occasions in show jumping competitions.

Weldon, Lt.-Col. Frank (b. 1913) G.B. Lt.-Col. Weldon is now the director of the Badminton Horse Trials and designs the cross-country course. He is also on the Combined Training Committee of the British Horse Society. In the early days of Britain's participation in Three-Day Events he was one of our most successful riders. In 1955, riding his brilliant horse Kilbarry, he became Individual European Champion. In 1956 he captained the British Olympic team at Stockholm which won the Team Gold Medal and he himself took the Individual Bronze. That same year he also won the Badminton Horse Trials with Kilbarry. He was in the team which won the European Championship for Britain in 1953, 1954, 1955 and 1957. He served in the King's Troop which he commanded from 1949–1954. In his pre-war days he rode in many point-to-point races and also under National Hunt rules. He is equestrian correspondent for the *Sunday Telegraph*. Lives very near Badminton, at Wickwar in Gloucestershire.

West, Debbie (b. 1949) G.B. Lives at Chiddingfold in Sussex and is one of Britain's most consistent Horse Trials riders. In 1972 with her chestnut, Baccarat, was a member of the British Olympic team at Munich. A few hours before the Three-Day Event was due to start Baccarat was found to have damaged his leg and she had to withdraw from the team. The previous year she had been runner-up to Princess Anne for the individual title in the European Championships at Burghley. In 1972, also at Burghley, was again 2nd, this time to Janet

Hodgson on Larkspur. She started her Eventing career when she was 17, competing at Tidworth on a mare called Island Dancer. After that she soon came to prominence with Don Camillo on which she was seldom unplaced.

Whiteley, Martin (b. 1930) G.B.   Now a schoolmaster at Eton, Capt. Whiteley served with the Greenjackets. He injured his back racing, so took up Eventing, and has the unique record of having completed the Badminton course eleven times on eight different horses. His greatest horse was The Poacher on whom he rode as a member of the British team for the World Championships at Burghley in 1966 and was placed 5th individually. In 1965 he won at Badminton, and in 1967 was 2nd individually in the European Championships in Ireland and a member of the winning British team.

Willcox, Sheila (b. 1936) G.B.   One of the greatest women Trials riders of all time until her career was ended by a broken back after a fall at Tidworth in 1971. For a time she was paralysed but eventually fought her way back to health and now, although no longer competing on cross-country courses, she rides in international dressage competitions and coaches Three-Day Event riders. It was undoubtedly Sheila Willcox who made the committee of the Olympic Games change their rule about admitting women as members of Three-Day Event teams. She is the only rider ever to have won Badminton in three successive years (Capt. Mark Phillips has won it three times but with a break between the victories), which she did in 1957, 1958 and 1959 – having missed victory in 1956 by only 1.56 points. She became European Champion in 1957 and in 1955 won at Turin. It was after her third Badminton victory that the Olympic Committee changed their rule. Ironically, although she had in the meantime won 'Little Badminton' in 1963 and come 3rd in 1964 – she was not chosen for the Olympic team that went to Tokyo. Britain sent an all-male team. (The honour of being the first woman to compete in an Olympic Three-Day Event fell to an American, Helen du Pont. At the next Olympics in 1968 in Mexico Britain did include a woman in the team, Jane Bullen, the 'galloping nurse'.)

Willson, Diana (b. 1934) EIRE First rode in senior Horse Trials in 1960 and also competes in show jumping competitions. Was a member of the Irish team which came 3rd in the European Championships at Burghley in 1971. In the World Championships at Punchestown in 1970 she finished 7th individually. On each of these occasions she was riding a horse called Broken Promise. She considers her best horse was Chianti Rossi on which she won the Punchestown Open Event in 1968, and finished 26th overall in the Olympic Games in Mexico as a member of the Irish team.

THE GREAT HORSES

As in the world of racing, so in the world of show jumping and Horse Trials, every so often a horse appears which captures the public imagination and becomes a 'personage' in his own right. Sometimes he is inevitably linked with one rider – they may indeed have risen to fame together. Other horses, however, have found glory with several riders, and have helped those riders on the way to fame. Inevitably there is not space in this volume to do honour to them all. The following pages pay tribute to a few, while not forgetting the many others who, had space permitted, should have been included.

Askan A grey gelding bought by Harvey Smith and Trevor Banks from Germany in 1974. In 1971, after being in the winning German Nations Cup teams at Rome and Fontainebleau (ridden by Paul Schockemohle), he was sold to Herr Kun for a reputed £56,000. This was then a record price for a show jumper. Askan was then taken over by Gerd Wiltfang. That year at Hickstead he won the Wills International Grand Prix and the Wills Embassy Stakes, and the following week at the Royal International Horse Show won the King George V Gold Cup. He went on to win the Player-Wills Men's Championship in Dublin and was in the winning German Nations Cup team. In 1972 Askan won the German International Championship at Aachen and was in the Olympic Gold Medal-winning German team at Munich. He was taken over by Alwin Schockemohle but the partnership was not a great success and eventually the horse was sold (at an undisclosed price) to the Harvey Smith–Trevor Banks partnership.

Barberry The horse on which triple Olympic medallist Richard Meade first came to international fame in the world of Horse Trials. Foaled in 1955 by Beauford out of Caraway Seed, this 16 h.h. (162 cm) horse was bred in Ireland. Richard Meade acquired him in 1961 and they competed together for the first time at Crookham the following year. Later in 1962 they won the Open at Tidworth and the Open Intermediate at Chatsworth, and this led to their first inclusion in a British team abroad, when they went to Munich in 1963. In 1964, having won at Eridge and Burghley, they were selected for the British team for the Tokyo Olympics. In 1965 they went to Moscow with the British team for the European Championships where the team came 3rd, and in 1966 Barberry won the Silver Medal in the World Championships (ridden as usual by Richard Meade) at Burghley. In 1967 they were in the team which won the European Championship at Punchestown and in 1968 were short-listed for the Mexico Olympics, but Barberry injured his back in a fall and his name had to be withdrawn. Shortly afterwards he was retired from competitive Trials.

Beethoven This 16 h.h. (162 cm) black gelding was bought as an unbroken 3-year-old in Ireland by Douglas Bunn. The horse had never been ridden, but early in 1962 Bunn broke him in and soon had him jumping 1.37 m (4 ft 6 in.) fences. By the end of the season he had won the Foxhunter Championship at Wembley. By the following year Bunn was riding him in winning Nations Cup teams, at Ostend in 1963, 1964 and 1965, and at Olsztyn in Poland in 1965, and in Nice in 1967. In 1965 Beethoven was runner-up for the King George V Gold Cup to the great Hans Winkler of Germany on Fortun. In 1970 *(below)* Tony Newbery, the young Devon international amateur rider, with his former Australian Olympic horse, Warwick

(far below) Harvey Smith on one of his most successful horses, Salvador, takes the water jump at Hickstead.

(*above*) Graham Fletcher, one of our leading amateurs, on Tauna Dora.

(*left*) Marion Mould on the leading horse of her present string, Dunlynne, who has won many important competitions.

(*below*) Lucinda Prior-Palmer on Be Fair. They became the European Champions in 1975. They have also won Badminton and the Midland Bank National Championship; and rode for Britain at Kiev in 1973.

(*far below*) German ace Hartwig Steenken on the great mare Simona. They became World Champions in 1974.

Bunn lent the horse to David Broome to ride in the Men's World Championship and the pair pulled off the title. Beethoven, now retired to the pastures around Hickstead, was always a great favourite with the crowd for his tail-swishing exuberant style, reminiscent of an earlier favourite, Vibart.

Cornishman V Originally bought by Brigadier D. M. L. Gordon-Watson of Dorset as a potential hunter, he was bred, as his name implies, in Cornwall in 1959. When the Gordon-Watsons first bought him, they found him a difficult and temperamental horse, albeit endowed with a great jump. At first the brigadier rode him and he won the Army Trophy in the Melton Cross-country. In 1966 it was decided to try him as an Event horse, and Mary, the brigadier's daughter, took him on and first rode him in a senior Event in 1966 in the novice class at Wylye. Two years later, he was in the Gold Medal-winning team for Britain at the Mexico Olympics, ridden by Richard Meade to whom he had been lent when Richard's horse, Barberry, broke down. In 1969, with Mary back in his saddle, the pair became Individual European Champions (Mary had been considered not experienced enough to be included in the team) at Haras du Pin in Normandy. In 1970, this time in the British team, they took the Individual World Championship held that year in Ireland, and helped the team win the Gold Medal. In 1971 they were 2nd at Badminton and in the British team which won the European Championship held that year at Burghley. In 1972 they were in the British team which won the Gold Medal at the Olympic Games.

Countryman III Foaled in Ireland in 1948, this dark brown gelding, 16.2 h.h. (164 cm) was bought by Event rider, Bertie Hill, from a dealer's yard in

Exeter in late 1952. At first he was raced (Bertie Hill was top amateur point to point rider in 1965) and as a 5-year-old won once and was 2nd twice. In 1954 he started to compete in Trials and in 1955 made his first international appearance as a member of the winning British team in the European Championships held that year in Windsor Great Park. In 1956 he was bought by H.M. The Queen and was the first Event horse she had owned. Later she sold him to the Duke of Beaufort. He was in the Gold Medal-winning team (ridden by Bertie Hill) in the Olympic Games at Stockholm in 1956. After the Duke of Beaufort took him over, he was ridden by the duke's heir, the Hon. David Somerset, at Badminton in 1957, 1958 and 1959. On the last occasion he was 2nd.

Craven A   This mare was one of the most famous show jumpers of the 1950s when Peter Robeson was first starting out on his international career. She was bred in Sussex by Peter Robeson's father who had also been an international show jumper. In 1952 she was the reserve horse for the British Olympic team at Helsinki. She was in the British teams at Le Zoute in 1949, Lucerne and Dublin in 1950, Le Zoute, Nice, Dublin and Rome in 1951, and after that in all the major Nations Cup events abroad, one of her busiest years being 1954 when she was at Lisbon, Madrid, London and Dublin, followed by Paris in 1955. She won the Victor Ludorum and the Fred Foster Cup for puissance in 1952 at the Horse of the Year Show, and again won the Fred Foster Cup in 1956. In 1954 she had a triple triumph, winning the Lonsdale Championship, puissance, and the Daily Mail Cup at the Royal International Horse Show. She was retired from competitive show jumping in the late 1950s, having helped Peter Robeson establish himself as one of the world's most stylish horsemen, and Britain as one of the leading show jumping countries.

Doublet   Bred by H.M. The Queen in 1963 as a polo pony, by Doubtless out of Swate, this 16.2 h.h. (164 cm) chestnut grew too big for polo and was handed over to Princess Anne who was beginning to make her mark in the world of Horse Trials. He proved to be a brilliant but tragic horse. In 1969 he won his first Trials at Windsor and two years later he finished 5th at Badminton. On the strength of this and other good results, he and Princess Anne were selected to ride for Britain as individuals in the European Championships in 1971 which were held that year at Burghley. They won the championship with a magnificent lead of 38 points and they seemed set for a place in the British Olympic team in Munich the following year. But early in the year, before Badminton, in fact, Doublet went lame and was out of action for a year. He returned to training in 1973 and was short-listed for the European Championships which that year were held in Kiev in Russia. Unfortunately, at the Trials at Osberton, where the final selection was to be made, he stopped at a difficult fence and was not selected. Later that year, at Wylye, he broke a blood vessel and had to be withdrawn. In 1974, while Princess Anne was exercising him in Windsor Great Park, he broke a leg and had to be destroyed.

Durlas Eile   One of the best-known ever Irish Eventers, this dark brown gelding was foaled in 1956 by Artist's Son out of Royal Cob, and sold as a 5-year-old to the Irish Army. In 1964 he was bought by Major Eddie Boylan of the Irish Equestrian team who came 4th with him at Burghley that year. In 1965, only eight months after they joined forces, they won Badminton, having led in every section. That same year they were in the

Irish team which came 2nd in the European Championships held in Moscow. In 1966 Durlas Eile and Boylan won the King's Cup, the services jumping award at the Royal Tournament, and the same year were in the winning Irish team at the World Championships held then, as in 1974, at Burghley. In 1967 they won the European Championship individual title at Punchestown in their native Ireland. After that Durlas Eile was sold to Canada for the then record price for an Eventer of £19,000, and was ridden in the Canadian team for the Mexico Olympics.

Flanagan One of the show jumpers which, together with his great partner, Pat Smythe, did so much to put British show jumping on the map in the 1950s and early '60s. A chestnut gelding, 16.1 h.h. (163 cm), he started life as a racehorse, then progressed to Eventing, and in 1954, aged 7, he was bought by Mr Robert Hanson, the great patron of show jumping from Yorkshire. Mr Hanson asked Pat Smythe to ride the horse and eventually, because of all the success she had achieved, he gave Flanagan to her in 1965. She rode him in the Stockholm Olympics in 1956 when Britain won the Bronze Medal for show jumping. In 1955, 1958 and 1962 they won the Ladies National Championship, and in 1962 won the British Jumping Derby and the Leading Show Jumper of the Year title at Wembley. Pat Smythe rode him to win the Ladies European Championship four times, at Spa in 1957, Deauville in 1961, Madrid in 1962, and Hickstead in 1963. He was in the winning British Nations Cup teams in Lucerne, Stockholm, London and Rotterdam in 1956; London and Harrisburg in 1957; and Madrid and Rotterdam in 1959. He was retired in 1966.

Foxhunter Probably the best-known show jumper

141

of all time and one which became a legendary figure in his lifetime. He represented Britain no less than thirty-five times in international shows, and as far back as 1948 helped to win a Team Bronze Medal at the Olympics in London. He won the King George V Gold Cup three times, in 1948, 1950 and 1953. At the Olympic Games in Helsinki in 1952, Britain won the Gold Medal for show jumping and it was Foxhunter who clinched the win by his last round in the team event. He not only won in Europe but made successful forays to New York and Toronto. He was always ridden by Lt-Col. Harry Llewellyn who perpetuated his name when he suggested the 'Foxhunter' novice championship competition, which today is the biggest competition in the world; thousands enter every year and the finals are held at the Horse of the Year Show. He died in 1959. Foxhunter's skeleton is now at the Royal College of Veterinary Surgeons in London.

Franco Owned by Robert Hanson. He started as a racehorse but became internationally famous as a show jumper, ridden first by David Barker, and at the end of 1966 by Caroline Bradley. He was in the winning British Nations Cup teams in 1962 at Lucerne, and in 1967 at Olsztyn and at Leipzig. In 1968 he won the Open Championship in Toronto and between 1962 and 1967 won individual honours at Dublin, Rome, Rotterdam, Ostend and Geneva.

Goodbye III Foaled in 1953 and bred in Ireland, he was ridden by one of Ireland's most popular and successful riders, Seamus Hayes, from 1960 until he was retired in 1967. In 1961 he won the first British Jumping Derby at Hickstead and repeated the feat in 1964 – the first horse to win twice. He won many individual international honours particularly at

142

Geneva, Ostend, Aachen, Dublin and London. In 1965 he won the Daily Mail Cup in London. In 1963 he was a member of the winning Irish team which took the Nations Cup at the Dublin Horse Show.

Goodwill   A 16.2 h.h. (164 cm) brown gelding now owned by H.M. The Queen and ridden by Princess Anne. He started competitive life by winning the Watney Mann Working Hunter of the Year Championship at the Horse of the Year Show in 1969 ridden by Miss Rita Burch. Then Alison Dawes took him over as a show jumper and he represented Britain in the Barcelona and Aachen International Shows. In 1972 H.M. The Queen bought him and Princess Anne started to 'Event' him. In 1973 she rode him at Kiev in Russia, competing as an individual to defend her title (won in 1971 at Burghley) in the European Championships. A fall, however, put them out of the competition and she lost the title. In 1974 they finished 4th at Badminton, and were selected to compete as individuals in the World Championships at Burghley when they finished 12th. Was in the British Silver Medal-winning team for the European Championship in 1975.

Great Ovation   Foaled in 1963, this 16.3 h.h. (165 cm) bay gelding is by Three Cheers out of Cyprus Valence. Owned jointly by Capt. Mark Phillips and his aunt, Miss Flavia Phillips, the horse started Eventing in 1971 when he had his first win at Rushall with Capt. Mark Phillips. They went on to win Badminton that year and repeated the feat in 1972. Unfortunately, an attempt to complete the hat trick in 1973 failed when Great Ovation went lame after the Steeplechase and had to be withdrawn. They were in the winning European Championship team for Britain at

Burghley in 1971 and were 6th individually. In 1972 they were in the British Olympic team at Munich when Britain won the Gold Medal in the Three-Day Event.

High and Mighty   Foaled in 1947, this was the horse which brought Eventing fame to Sheila Willcox who was still in her teens when she bought him in 1954. The following year he made his début in Three-Day Eventing at no less challenging an occasion than the European Championships, held that year in Windsor Great Park. He competed as an individual and finished 13th out of fifty-four starters from many countries over a course so tough that only two teams finished. Later that year he was 4th at the now defunct Harewood Trials which have been replaced by Burghley. After this performance the pair were invited to train in the British team for an international Three-Day Event to be held in Turin. Not only did the British team win, but High and Mighty was overall individual winner. He won Badminton twice in succession in 1957 and 1958, the first horse ever to do so, and won the European Championship in 1957 at Copenhagen as well as being in the winning British team. Sheila Willcox retired him in 1958 and he concentrated on dressage. He died in 1969.

Irish Cap   A bay gelding which became World Champion in the Three-Day Event at Burghley in 1974 for the U.S.A., ridden by Bruce Davidson from Westport, Massachusetts. Earlier in that season, he had been placed 3rd at Badminton and had competed successfully in Combined Training Events at the Royal International Horse Show at Wembley.

Kilbarry   Another of the great Event horses. Owned by Lt-Col. Frank Weldon, this grey gelding

is probably the only horse to win international
Eventing fame while doing his full daily duty as an
officer's charger with the King's Troop R.H.A. 'A
proper soldier's horse' was how Lt-Col. Weldon
described him. He won his first Trials as a novice in
1953 at Stowell Park. When the European
Championships were held at Badminton in 1953
he was in the winning British team (no other team
finished) and came 2nd individually. In 1954 they
were in the winning British team for the European
Championships at Basle and again came 2nd
individually. They were 2nd at Badminton that
year. In 1955 they became European Champions
and again were in the winning British team, this
time at Windsor, the third successive time they had
been in a winning team. They won an Olympic
Team Gold Medal at Stockholm in 1956 and an
Individual Bronze. In 1957 Kilbarry broke his
neck at a small One-Day Event.

Mattie Brown An Irish-bred, chestnut gelding,
16.1 h.h. (163 cm), ridden by Harvey Smith –
although he has changed owners, and names, since
he was brought over to Britain in 1967. He is the
only horse to have won the British Jumping Derby
in two successive years, which he did in 1970 and
1971. When he was first brought over from Ireland
he was called Condor, then he was sold to John
Player and Sons and renamed Doncella. Later he
was sold again, this time to Mr J. B. Eastwood, and
renamed yet again – Mattie Brown. As well as the
British Jumping Derby, he also won the King
George V Gold Cup at the Royal International
Horse Show in 1970 and the Grand Prix of Ireland
in Dublin. The same year Harvey Smith rode him
in the World Championships, held at La Baule in
France, and was placed 3rd. He has been in
winning Nations Cup teams in Dublin and

Hickstead. At home he has won many of the top classes at major shows.

Merely-a-Monarch By Happy Monarch out of Merely a Mind, this 16.2 h.h. (164 cm) dark brown gelding was always ridden by Anneli Drummond-Hay (now Mrs Wucherphennig and living in South Africa). There was a brief period when his ownership changed to Mr Robert Hanson, but after a court case as to who should ride him, he was sold back to Anneli and she then owned him jointly with Lt-Col. T. Greenhalgh. He was first brought out as an Eventer and won at Burghley in 1961 and Badminton in 1962. After this he entered for show jumping only (he had in fact come 4th in the final of the Daily Express Foxhunter Championship at Wembley in 1960) and had a distinguished career. With him Anneli Drummond-Hay became European Ladies Champion in 1968 in Rome, and in 1970 was 3rd in the Ladies World Championship at Copenhagen. That year they also won the Queen Elizabeth II Cup at the Royal International Show. Abroad he won many major individual honours including the Canadian Grand Prix in Toronto in 1966, the Grand Prix of Monaco and the Grand Prix of Switzerland in Geneva, both in 1967. He was in winning British teams in Rome, London and Nice between 1963 and 1970.

Mr Banbury For most show jumping enthusiasts this horse will always be thought of by his original name of The Maverick. It was changed in 1973 by his owner and rider, Mrs Alison Dawes, when she turned professional and was sponsored by a building firm. This bay gelding, 16 h.h. (162 cm), has twice won the British Jumping Derby (once under each name), in 1968 and in 1973. He was reserve horse for the 1968 Olympics in Mexico. He won the Queen Elizabeth II Cup in 1969 and was also joint winner with Psalm (ridden by Ann Moore) in 1973. Mrs Dawes was Ladies National Champion with him in 1969 and 1972, runner-up for the Ladies European Championship at St Gallen in 1971, and 3rd in the Ladies World Championship in 1965. He has won major competitions on both sides of the Atlantic and has been in winning British Nations Cup teams in 1965, 1971 and 1972. He was originally purchased in Ireland as a 7-year-old in 1962 by Mr Douglas Bunn and was sold to Mrs Dawes in 1963. He died early in 1975, a few weeks after his retirement ceremony at the 1974 Dunhill Christmas Show at Olympia.

Mister Softee A chestnut gelding owned by Mr John Massarella and first registered with the B.S.J.A. in 1960, he was one of the great show jumping horses of the 1960s. He had three riders, David Barker, John Lanni and David Broome, but his greatest triumphs came during his partnership with Broome which started in 1965. He won the European Championship three times, in 1962 (ridden by David Barker) and in 1967 and 1969 ridden by David Broome. In the 1968 Olympics at Mexico he and Broome won an Individual Bronze Medal. 1966 was possibly his greatest year, for in it he won the British Jumping Derby, the King George V Gold Cup, and the Victor Ludorum for the Ronson Trophy at the Horse of the Year Show, apart from various championships in the north of England. Abroad he won championships in Dublin, Rotterdam, Rome and Geneva. He was retired from international competition in 1970.

Pennwood Forge Mill One of the greatest show jumpers of the 1970s, this horse was as much a favourite with the crowd as his rider, Paddy McMahon. He is owned by Mr Fred Hartill of Wolverhampton who at one time was offered – and refused – £80,000 for him. The first success McMahon had with him was in 1971 when they won the John Eastwood Men's Championship at the Rothman's Show Jumping Championships at Lincoln. In 1972 they were the top money winners of the season, taking more than £7,000. They won the Saddle of Honour at the Royal International Horse Show as the most consistent combination and were short-listed for the 1972 Olympics at Munich – but were not finally selected. They were 2nd that year in the British Jumping Derby and in the B.S.J.A. National Championships, then won the Victor Ludorum at the Horse of the Year Show in a competition which had the audience on its feet as they raced to a tenth of a second's victory against the reigning European Champion, Hartwig Steenken (later in 1974 to become World Champion). In 1973 the pair won the Men's European Championship at Hickstead and the following week, at the Royal International Show, they won the King George V Gold Cup and the Horse and Hound Cup. In 1974 he was selected to jump for Britain in the Men's World Championship and was among the leaders for the first two 'legs'. In the third and final phase he dropped back, unaccountably, at the time, but later, when his disappointed owner had him X-rayed, he was found to have injured a neck muscle.

Playamar A bay gelding, 16.1 h.h. (163 cm), sired by Shelley's Boy, owned and ridden by Hugh Thomas from Basingstoke, Hants, who was the Individual Bronze Medallist in the 1974 World Three-Day Event Championship at Burghley, the highest placed of any individual British rider, though not a member of the team which won the Silver Medal. Earlier in 1974 Playamar had been placed 8th at Badminton, and in 1973 was a member of the British team at Boekelo in Holland.

Psalm A 16 h.h. (162 cm) brown gelding thoroughbred, ridden by Ann Moore, who retired from show jumping in 1974 at the age of 23 when Psalm had to give up show jumping owing to leg injury. His finest achievement was in 1972 when he and Ann won the Individual Silver Medal at the Olympics in Munich. His sire was Sermon and he was foaled in 1960. He was sold to the Moores in 1966 and by 1968 was fully launched on his great career, having already won, with Ann, the Young Riders Championship of Great Britain in 1967. In 1968 the pair won that championship again, and also the National Young Riders Championship and the Leading Young Rider of the Year Championship. In the same year Ann rode him to become Junior European Champion and he was a member of the winning British team in the championships. In 1970 he competed successfully in an adult competition in Madrid and was a member of the winning British Nations Cup team at Ostend. In 1971 Psalm was one of two horses Ann rode to become European Ladies Champion at St Gall. As well as the Olympic Silver Medal they also won in 1972 the Queen Elizabeth II Cup, the Wills Derby Trial at Hickstead and the Wills Grand Prix Bristol Trophy. In 1973 they tied for 1st place with Mrs Dawes on Mr Banbury in the Queen Elizabeth II Cup and Ann Moore retained her Ladies European title in Vienna.

Salvador A German-bred horse brought to this country by Harvey Smith in partnership with Trevor Banks. On him Harvey won the Wills British Jumping Derby in 1974 and they rode together in a number of winning British Nations Cup teams abroad. In 1973 he was one of the top ten national and international horses in the list of prize money winners. At the Royal International Horse Show in 1974 he helped Harvey Smith win his first Victor Ludorum for the Daily Mail Cup.

Simona A German Hanoverian mare foaled in 1958 on which Hartwig Steenken became World Champion at Hickstead in 1974. Steenken also rode her in the 1972 Olympics at Munich when Germany won the Team Gold Medal. In 1971 they won the Men's European title, but Steenken broke his leg in 1973 and was unable to defend his title.

Stroller Probably the most amazing little horse of modern times. At 14.2 h.h. (144 cm), this bay gelding was really a pony, and indeed started his official career in 1961 with Marion Mould, then Marion Coakes, when she was 14 and he was 9, competing in junior Foxhunter classes. He had been purchased from Sally Cripps who first registered him with the B.S.J.A. in 1958. Within four years of starting his career with Marion in junior classes, he had partnered her to win the Ladies World Championship at Hickstead in 1965. She was then only just 18, and already they had been in winning British teams in Poland, Dublin and Copenhagen, besides taking almost every major prize at home. In 1968 they were members of the British team for the Olympic Games in Mexico, where they won the Individual Silver Medal for Britain, beaten only by the tremendously experienced Snowbound of America, ridden by Bill Steinkraus. The previous year they won the British Jumping Derby at Hickstead, and in 1965 and 1971 they won the Queen Elizabeth II Cup at the Royal International Horse Show. They hold the record for winning the Hickstead Gold Medal (given by W. D. and H. O. Wills for the horse and rider scoring the most points in the season) no less than five successive times. Stroller also had wins in New York, Rome, Hamburg and Rotterdam besides winning almost every major trophy at home, and between 1962 and 1972 almost every major championship. When he officially retired in 1973 there was a special ceremony for him at Hickstead which had been the scene of so many of his triumphs.

Sunsalve   This was the mount of David Broome when he won the King George V Gold Cup in 1960 and a few months later an Individual Bronze Medal at the Rome Olympics. They also won the Men's European Championship in 1961 at Aachen. Before he was Broome's mount, however, he had already started on a distinguished career. He was owned by Mr Oliver Anderson of Dereham in Norfolk and originally ridden by Mr Anderson's daughter, Elizabeth. On him she won the Brighton Centenary Gold Cup for Ladies in 1955 and 1957, and in 1957 also won the Queen Elizabeth II Gold Cup. Sunsalve is the only horse to date ever to win both the Queen Elizabeth II and the King George V Gold Cups. When Elizabeth Anderson gave up riding, he was at first leased to the British team for Pat Smythe to ride, and then handed over to David Broome. Sunsalve died of heart failure in 1962 when little more than 12 years old.

The Maverick VII, *see* Mr Banbury

The Poacher   A bay gelding, 16.2 h.h. (164 cm), one of the toughest Three-Day Event horses ever trained, and yet he started life as a hunter, being ridden side-saddle by Mrs Phyllis Tomkinson. She had bought him from Miss Shelagh Kesler, a well-known west country judge of a horse who had found him in Exeter market. Eventually, when Mrs Tomkinson gave up riding him he was sold back to Miss Kesler and competed in show jumping competitions. Mr Martin Whiteley, an Eton schoolmaster, who was one of our most distinguished Event riders until a back injury forced him to retire, bought The Poacher and decided to train him as an Eventer. He immediately made his mark, not only when ridden by his owner but also by his trainer, Michael Herbert. Among his victories were 1st place in the Little Badminton Event and 1st at Chatsworth; later, in 1966, he was 5th in the World Championships at Burghley, and in 1967 was 2nd individually and also a member of the winning British team in the European Championships in Ireland, ridden by his owner. At the Olympic Games in Mexico in 1968 he was handed over to the Combined Training Committee of the British Horse Society who were asked to provide a rider as Martin Whiteley's back was causing him trouble; he was ridden by Staff-Sgt Ben Jones who was placed 5th overall and helped Britain win the Team Gold Medal. In 1969 he was a member of the European Gold Medal-winning team in France. In 1970, ridden by Richard Meade, he won the Badminton Horse Trials and was a member of the British Gold Medal-winning team in the World Championships at Punchestown in Ireland. In 1971, again partnered by Richard Meade, he was in the winning British team in the European Championships and was placed 6th overall. After this he was retired.

The Rock   Foaled in 1948, this grey gelding was one of the best-known foreign horses to compete regularly in Britain, ridden by Piero d'Inzeo, the elder of the two famous Italian brothers. Like so many wonderful show jumpers, he was bred in Ireland. Was purchased in the early part of the 1950s for the Italian Equestrian Federation and in 1957 first came to British public notice when he cleared 2.15 m (7 ft 1 in.) in the Moss Bros Championship for puissance at the Royal International Horse Show. In 1960 at the Rome Olympics he won an Individual Silver Medal, and altogether he won more than 170 first prizes at nearly fifty international shows, including the King George V Gold Cup in London in 1962. He was in Nations Cup team wins for Italy from 1960 to 1966 in Turin, London, Rome, Nice and Aachen. Towards the end of his career he was ridden by Graciano Mancinelli, another of Italy's great international riders. He died in 1966.

Untouchable   One of the best-known American show jumpers of all time. This chestnut gelding, 16.1 h.h. (163 cm), started life as a racehorse but was sold to Mr and Mrs Patrick Butler, after being discovered by the late Ben O'Meara, one of America's leading professional riders. Handed over to Kathy Kusner, the show jumper and leading lady jockey (one of the few who holds a full flat-racing licence), he twice won the Dublin Grand Prix (1964 and 1965), was runner-up in the Ladies World Championship at Hickstead in 1965, won the Canadian Championship in 1967, and many other international awards in Ostend, Rotterdam, Germany, Switzerland, London, Dublin, Toronto and New York. He was also in the winning U.S.A. Nations Cup teams on nine occasions between 1964 and 1968.

Wayfarer II   A 17 h.h. (173 cm) bay gelding owned by Mrs H. Wilkin and ridden by Richard Meade in the 1974 World Three-Day Event Championship when Britain won the Silver Medal. The couple won the Boekelo Three-Day Event in Holland in 1973 and were 8th at Badminton in 1974. Meade rode him in the European Championships at Kiev in 1973 when Britain was placed 3rd.

THE YOUNG GET STARTED:
THE PONY CLUB

Although people of any age can and do take up riding, and many continue strenuous hunting at considerably advanced years, show jumping and its sister sport of Eventing are normally sports for the fairly young, and those who start young have an infinite advantage. (There are, of course, notable exceptions in the show jumping world where several of the best-known professionals are well past their 40th and even 50th birthdays.)

The Pony Club, which started in Britain, offers the young unique opportunities of learning and gaining experience in all aspects of horsemanship. Youngsters are not only taught to ride and care for their ponies, but have their own rallies, camps, competitions, examinations, show jumping classes and Horse Trials. Great store is set on the working rallies, and besides actual riding, members take part in clipping and plaiting their ponies, bandaging and grooming, mucking-out and bedding-down, fitting and caring for saddlery, first aid and the many other practical duties which owning a pony involves. Other Pony Club activities include polo and tetrathlon (riding, running, shooting and swimming).

The movement has now spread to other countries, and is playing an ever increasing part in promoting international goodwill, sportsmanship, and friendly competition. It is represented in twenty countries and has a membership of more than 75,000 – the largest association of riders in the world.

Membership of the Pony Club is divided into two classes, 'ordinary' and 'associate'. 'Ordinary' members are boys and girls under the age of 17 and 'associate' members are those from 17 to 20. Membership must end when the rider reaches 20 years of age.

Any youngster who likes riding will find great fun and excitement through being a member of a branch of the Pony Club, but those who wish to make a career in show jumping will lay a foundation in their early years which is second to none. Almost without exception the great names in show jumping in Britain have all started as members of the Pony Club.

Among former members, either ordinary or associate, are H.R.H. The Princess Anne, former European Three-Day Event Champion; her husband, Olympic Gold Medallist, Capt. Mark Phillips; triple Olympic Gold Medallist, Richard Meade; Olympic Gold Medallist, Jane Bullen; former Ladies World Champion, Marion Mould; former World Champion, David Broome; and British National Champion (at only 17), Pip Nicholls.

Although membership may be continued up to the age of 20, youngsters cease to ride ponies after they are 16. This gives them a chance to get accustomed to riding horses while still retaining young riders' status, and to compete against riders of their own age groups while making the transition. Often this transition proves quite a difficult one. Ponies are long-lived creatures and go on in their jumping careers long after horses, so that a child often learns as much from an experienced pony as from any human mentor. The sort of horse on which a youngster usually starts – a novice – is not usually so sagacious, thus, not only is the rider having to get used to bigger jumps and distances, but is also having to train his mount. Often, too, parents find it difficult to know where to look for a suitable type of horse at a price they can afford. Fellow members of the Pony Club are sometimes able to help by pooling their knowledge.

Pony Club members wear a distinctive tie in the club colours of blue, gold and purple, and a hard hat is essential. In any Pony Club competition, if a competitor loses his hat and fails to replace it before continuing, he is eliminated. This rule helps to impress safety on the young. The Pony Club arranges for specially approved hats and saddles and other equipment to be supplied to members at special prices.

Although many branches of the Pony Club are affiliated to a local hunt in name, or have as their officials members of the local hunt, the Pony Club in no way compels its members to go hunting although those who wish to do so are given every encouragement. Some branches, such as those in the London area, have of course no connection with a hunt.

One of the chief sources of enjoyment for Pony Club members are the inter-branch competitions. Some of these, such as the Mounted Games for the Prince Philip Cup, take place in various stages, and the teams which do best compete for the final at the Horse of the Year Show at Wembley each autumn. This competition gives every member a chance to have fun but at the same time to compete seriously against other members in team games which involve well-schooled ponies though not necessarily high-quality animals.

The Pony Club runs an insurance scheme against legal liabilities for accidents to third parties or damage caused to property of third parties during official activities of any branch of the club, but does not cover personal insurance for accidents sustained by members, or insurance of ponies. These matters must be arranged, if required, by the individual members themselves. Further details of the Pony Club's scheme for insurance may be obtained from the headquarters of the club at the National Equestrian Centre, Stoneleigh, Kenilworth, Warwickshire, CV8 2LR.

In 1979 the Pony Club celebrates its Golden Jubilee, for it was back in 1929 that the Institute of the Horse (which was a fore-runner of the British Horse Society) inaugurated a junior branch, to be known as the 'Pony Club'. Its object was to interest 'young people in riding and sport and at the same time offer the opportunity of higher instruction in this direction than many of them could obtain individually'. The pattern of the badge issued then has remained unchanged.

In January 1930 the Central Committee held its first meeting and by the following May there were 700 members and the first overseas branch had been formed – the Royal Calpe Hunt Pony Club in Gibraltar. Within twelve months the membership had increased to 4,442 and there were 59 branches. The first Pony Club camp was held in 1931. By 1934 there were 103 branches and 8,350 members; Pony Club tests had been instituted and Pony Club Instructors' Courses were held for the first time.

During the Second World War almost every branch had to close down but the club was kept going by Mrs T. H. S. Marchant who carried out the secretarial duties for headquarters single-handed. However, in 1945, the Organization Committee met again under the chairmanship of Col., the Hon. C. G. Cubitt (who held the office of Chairman of the Pony Club until 1970).

By 1947 there were 167 branches of the Pony Club, with a membership of 17,082, and there were 13 overseas branches. The Pony Club came under the parent organization of the British Horse Society which was formed that year by the amalgamation of the Institute of the Horse and the

157

National Horse Association of Great Britain.

Gradually the activities of the Pony Club increased. First came the introduction of Horse Trials for members in addition to show jumping, and then in 1957 the Pony Club Mounted Games Championship with a cup given by Prince Philip. These games were to become as popular and widespread in the Pony Club as the Foxhunter novice jumping competitions were for adults. They eventually spread to many foreign countries. In 1958 polo was added to the club's activities.

The first exchange visit of Pony Club members from Britain to the United States took place in 1965, and in 1971 British members were hosts to Pony Club teams from Australia, Canada, Eire, South Africa and the United States. Now exchange visits have become a normal part of the activities of the club.

For administration purposes the Pony Club is divided into 'Districts' and 'Areas'. Areas consist of a number of districts, their boundaries corresponding as far as possible with those of the Sports Council Regions, though sometimes, owing to the size of the latter, two or more Pony Club areas are included within one Sports Council Region. Each district has a 'Commissioner' who elects an 'Area Representative'. The latter serves on the Pony Club Council during his or her term of office, but it is the commissioner who has the closest contact with the members. His duties include keeping a record of the dates of birth of all members in his branch, collecting fees and subscriptions, organizing rallies, lectures and other activities, and keeping simple accounts of financial affairs of the branch.

One excellent feature of the Pony Club is that although it has its own show jumping and Horse Trials championships, it does not encourage children to seek money prizes, and these are in fact

(*above*) A highlight of the Horse of the Year Show is the final of the Pony Club Mounted Games for the Prince Philip Cup in which the audience is as enthusiastic as the competitors.

(*below*) Clair Johnsey, at the age of 11, taking the pony stallion Champ over a double. Champ carried 'big sister' Debbie to the Junior European Championship in 1973.

(*above*) Peter Robeson, the doyen of the top-class international British riders, having first jumped in an Olympic team in 1956 at Stockholm.

(*right*) Paddy McMahon, former European Champion, on the great Pennwood Forge Mill.

(*above*) Janet Hodgson on Larkspur. Janet was elected Equestrian Personality of the Year by the British Equestrian Writers Association in 1973, the first year of the award.

(*left*) Triple Olympic Gold Medallist, Richard Meade, on Wayfarer owned by Mrs Henry Wilkin. Their wins include the Boekelo Three-Day Event in Holland in 1973.

forbidden for Pony Club competitions. This does not mean that youngsters never win cash prizes since they are always given for junior classes at horse shows, and members of the Pony Club can, and do, form the bulk of the entries at these classes. Ponies are graded for these shows according to the money they have won (*see* p. 30). To enter these competitions youngsters must be junior (or junior associate) members of the British Show Jumping Association and their ponies must be registered with, and be owned by members of, the Association.

According to the British Show Jumping Association rules no pony may exceed 14.2 h.h. (144 cm) with half an inch allowed for normal shoes. To compete as a junior, the rider must not have reached his (or her) 16th birthday on 1st January of the current year. An official height certificate, signed by an official measurer for the pony, and a birth certificate for the rider must be lodged with the association headquarters.

A junior rider who has reached the age of 14 may compete in junior competitions on a pony and in senior events on a horse. This is sometimes done by more outstanding young riders, who then pay an extra fee and become junior associate members of the British Show Jumping Association. If a youngster is really outstanding, however, he (or more often she) often opts out of junior grading altogether and concentrates on riding horses in senior or 'young riders' competitions.

The rules also permit a pony to be jumped in adult classes but in this case it may not compete in junior competitions as well, and must be re-registered as a horse. The most famous example of a pony competing in senior events was Stroller, the 14.2 h.h. (144 cm) pony which first won a junior Foxhunter competition in 1958, and in 1962 and 1963 was winning junior events with Marion

Coakes (later to become Mrs Marion Mould). Stroller then went on to senior events with her, gaining an individual Olympic Silver Medal in 1968, and the Ladies World Championship in 1965.

As there are more than 300 branches of the Pony Club in Britain it is impossible to list them all. The following, however, is a list of the Areas, and approximately the regions covered.

Area No. 1   Includes most of Scotland and Orkney

Area No. 2   Border counties and S. Scotland

Area No. 3   Lake District, Yorkshire, Durham

Area Nos 4   Lancashire, Cheshire, Isle of Man
and 5

Area No. 6   Nottinghamshire, Leicestershire,
              Lincolnshire

Area No. 7   Staffordshire, Shropshire,
              Warwickshire

Area No. 8   Cambridgeshire, Essex, Norfolk,
              Suffolk

Area No. 9   Cotswolds, Gloucestershire, South
              Hereford and Ross, Worcestershire
              and parts of Berkshire

Area No. 10   Radnor and Herefordshire, Welsh
              Borders

Area No. 11   Kent, S. London, Surrey, Sussex

Area No. 12   Hertfordshire, Middlesex, parts of
              Oxfordshire

Area No. 13   W. Surrey, Hampshire, parts of
              Berkshire, Isle of Wight

Area No. 14   Wiltshire, Dorset, New Forest, W.
              Hampshire, Isle of Wight

Pony Club badge

RECORDS

Badminton Horse Trials (Three-Day Event)

1949   John Shedden on *Golden Willow*, Gt Britain
1950   Capt. J. Collings on *Remus*, Gt Britain
1951   Capt. H. Schwarzenbach on *Vae Victis*, Switzerland
1952   Capt. M. A. Q. Darley on *Emily Little*, Gt Britain
1953   European Championships
1954   Miss M. Hough on *Bambi V*, Gt Britain
1955   European Championships
1956   Major Frank Weldon on *Kilbarry*, Gt Britain
1957   Miss Sheila Willcox on *High and Mighty*, Gt Britain
1958   Miss Sheila Willcox on *High and Mighty*, Gt Britain
1959   Mrs Sheila Waddington (née Willcox) on *Airs and Graces*, Gt Britain
1960   Bill Roycroft on *Our Solo*, Australia
1961   Laurie Morgan on *Salad Days*, Australia
1962   Miss Anneli Drummond-Hay on *Merely-a-Monarch*, Gt Britain
1963   Cancelled
1964   Capt. James Templer on *M'Lord Connolly*, Gt Britain
1965   Major Eddie Boylan on *Durlas Eile*, Ireland
1966   Cancelled
1967   Miss Celia Ross-Taylor on *Jonathan*, Gt Britain
1968   Miss Jane Bullen on *Our Nobby*, Gt Britain
1969   Richard Walker on *Pasha*, Gt Britain
1970   Richard Meade on *The Poacher*, Gt Britain
1971   Lt Mark Phillips on *Great Ovation*, Gt Britain
1972   Lt Mark Phillips on *Great Ovation*, Gt Britain
1973   Miss Lucinda Prior-Palmer on *Be Fair*, Gt Britain
1974   Capt. Mark Phillips on *Columbus*, Gt Britain
1975   Abandoned due to bad weather
1976
1977
1978
1979

British Jumping Derby

1961   Seamus Hayes on *Goodbye III*, Ireland
1962   Miss Pat Smythe on *Flanagan*, Gt Britain
1963   Nelson Pessoa on *Gran Geste*, Brazil
1964   Seamus Hayes on *Goodbye III*, Ireland
1965   Nelson Pessoa on *Gran Geste*, Brazil
1966   David Broome on *Mister Softee*, Gt Britain
1967   Miss Marion Coakes on *Stroller*, Gt Britain
1968   Miss Alison Westwood on *The Maverick VII*, Gt Britain
1969   Miss Anneli Drummond-Hay on *Xanthos*, Gt Britain

1970	Harvey Smith on *Mattie Brown*, Gt Britain
1971	Harvey Smith on *Mattie Brown*, Gt Britain
1972	Hendrik Snoek on *Shirokko*, W. Germany
1973	Mrs Alison Dawes (née Westwood) on *Mr Banbury* (*The Maverick VII*), Gt Britain
1974	Harvey Smith on *Salvador*, Gt Britain
1975	Paul Darragh on *Pele*, Ireland
1976	
1977	
1978	
1979	

British Show Jumping Association
Ladies National Championship

1948	Lady Dudley on *Princess*
1949	Miss Audrey Hinchcliffe on *Victory*
1950	Miss J. Makin on *Paddy V*
1951	Miss P. Rose on *Without Reserve*
1952	Miss Pat Smythe on *Prince Hal*
1953	Miss Pat Smythe on *Tosca*
1954	Miss Dawn Palethorpe on *Earlsrath Rambler*
1955	Miss Dawn Palethorpe on *Flanagan*
1956	Miss A. Morley on *Nugget*
1957	Miss Pat Smythe on *Prince Hal*
1958	Miss Pat Smythe on *Flanagan*
1959	Miss Pat Smythe on *Mr Pollard*
1960	Miss J. Shepherd on *Thou Swell*
1961	Miss Pat Smythe on *Scorchin*
1962	Miss Pat Smythe on *Flanagan*
1963	Miss A. Townsend on *Dunboyne*
1964	Miss Elizabeth Broome on *Bess*
1965	Cancelled
1966	Miss C. Warburton on *Nautilus II*
1967	Miss Jean Goodwin on *Hobo*
1968	Miss Jean Goodwin on *Hobo*
1969	Mrs Valerie Barker on *Brandy Jim*
1970	Miss Shirley Edwards on *Bright Morning*
1971	Miss Anne Coleman on *Havana Royal*
1972	Miss Alison Dawes on *The Maverick VII*
1973	Mrs A. Backhouse on *Cardinal*
1974	Miss Ann Moore on *Psalm*
1975	Mrs E. Edgar on *Everest Maybe*
1976	
1977	
1978	
1979	

British Show Jumping Association National Championship

1947	Lt-Col. N. H. Kindersley on *Maguire*
1948	Seamus Hayes on *Limerick*
1949	Seamus Hayes on *Sheila*
1950	Seamus Hayes on *Sheila*
1951	Alan Oliver on *Red Admiral* and *Red Knight*
1952	D. Beard on *Costa*
1953	Lt-Col. H. M. Llewellyn on *Foxhunter*
1954	Alan Oliver on *Red Admiral*
1955	Ted Williams on *Larry* and *Sunday Morning*
1956	Ted Williams on *Montana* and *Pegasus XIII*
1957	Ted Edgar on *Jane Summers*
1958	Paddy McMahon on *Tim II*
1959	Alan Oliver on *John Gilpin*
1960	Harvey Smith on *Farmer's Boy*
1961	David Broome on *Discutido*
1962	Tied:Pat Smythe on *Grand Manan* David Broome on *Wildfire III*
1963	Harvey Smith on *O'Malley*
1964	Miss E. Broome on *Jacopo*
1965	Peter Robeson on *Firecrest*
1966	Andrew Fielder on *Vibart*
1967	David Broome on *Mister Softee*
1968	Miss Marion Coakes on *Stroller*
1969	Alan Oliver on *Pitz Palu*
1970	Alan Oliver on *Sweep III*
1971	Mrs Marion Mould (née Coakes) on *Stroller*
1972	Miss Aileen Ross on *Trevarrion*
1973	David Broome on *Sportsman*
1974	Pip Nicholls on *Timmie*
1975	Harvey Smith on *Speak Easy*
1976	
1977	
1978	
1979	

Burghley Horse Trials (Three-Day Event)

1961	Miss Anneli Drummond-Hay on *Merely-a-Monarch*, Gt Britain
1962	European Championships
1963	Capt. Harry Freeman-Jackson on *St Finbarr*, Ireland
1964	Richard Meade on *Barberry*, Gt Britain
1965	Capt. Jeremy Beale on *Victoria Bridge*, Gt Britain
1966	World Championships
1967	Miss Lorna Sutherland on *Popadom*, Gt Britain
1968	Miss Sheila Willcox on *Fair and Square*, Gt Britain

1969	Miss Gillian Watson on *Shaitan*, Gt Britain
1970	Miss Judy Bradwell on *Don Camillo*, Gt Britain
1971	European Championships
1972	Miss Janet Hodgson on *Larkspur*, Gt Britain
1973	Capt. Mark Phillips on *Maid Marion*, Gt Britain
1974	World Championships
1975	Aly Pattison on *Carawich*, Gt Britain
1976	
1977	
1978	
1979	

EUROPEAN CHAMPIONSHIPS – SHOW JUMPING
Ladies European Championship

1957	*Spa*	1st Miss Pat Smythe on *Flanagan*, Gt Britain
		2nd Miss G. Serventi on *Doly*, Italy
		3rd Mrs M. d'Orgeix on *Ocean*, France
1958	*Palermo*	1st Miss G. Serventi on *Doly*, Italy
		2nd Miss A. Clement on *Nico*, W. Germany
		3rd Miss I. Jansen on *Adelbloom*, Holland
1959	*Rotterdam*	1st Miss Ann Townsend on *Bandit*, Gt Britain
		2nd Miss Pat Smythe on *Flanagan*, Gt Britain
		3rd Tied: Miss G. Serventi on *Doly*, Italy
		Miss A. Clement on *Nico*, W. Germany
1960	*Copenhagen*	1st Miss Sue Cohen on *Clare Castle*, Gt Britain
		2nd Mrs D. Wofford on *Hollandia*, Gt Britain
		3rd Miss A. Clement on *Nico*, W. Germany
1961	*Deauville*	1st Miss Pat Smythe on *Flanagan*, Gt Britain
		2nd Miss I. Jansen on *Icare*, Holland
		3rd Miss M. Cancre on *Ocean*, France
1962	*Madrid*	1st Miss Pat Smythe on *Flanagan*, Gt Britain
		2nd Mrs H. Kohler on *Cremona*, W. Germany
		3rd Mrs P. de Goyoaga on *Kif Kif*, Spain [Gt Britain
1963	*Hickstead*	1st Miss Pat Smythe on *Flanagan*,

169

		2nd Mrs A. Givaudan on *Huipil*, Brazil
		3rd Miss Anneli Drummond-Hay on *Merely-a-Monarch*, Gt Britain
1964	*No competition*	
1965	*Ladies World Championship*	
1966	*Gijon*	1st Miss Janou Lefebvre on *Kenavo*, France
		2nd Miss Monica Bachmann on *Sandro*, Switzerland
		3rd Miss Lalla Novo on *Oxo Bob*, Italy
1967	*Fontainebleau*	1st Miss Kathy Kusner on *Untouchable*, U.S.A.
		2nd Miss Lalla Novo on *Predestine*, Italy
		3rd Miss Monica Bachmann on *Erbach*, Switzerland
1968	*Rome*	1st Miss Anneli Drummond-Hay on *Merely-a-Monarch*, Gt Britain
		2nd Miss G. Serventi on *Gay Monarch*, Italy
		3rd Tied: Miss Marion Coakes on *Stroller*, Gt Britain
		Miss Janou Lefebvre on *Rocket*, France
1969	*Dublin*	1st Miss Iris Kellett on *Morning Light*, Ireland
		2nd Miss Anneli Drummond-Hay on *Xanthos*, Gt Britain
		3rd Miss Alison Westwood on *The Maverick VII*, Gt Britain
1970	*No competition*	
1971	*St Gallen*	1st Miss Ann Moore on *Psalm*, Gt Britain
		2nd Mrs Alison Dawes (née Westwood) on *The Maverick VII*, Gt Britain
		3rd Miss M. Leitenberger on *Limbarra de Porto Conte*, Austria
1972	*No competition*	
1973	*Vienna*	1st Miss Ann Moore on *Psalm*, Gt Britain
		2nd Miss Caroline Bradley on *True Lass*, Gt Britain
		3rd Mrs P. Weier on *Erbach*, Switzerland

(After 1973 only one title in this championship, open to either sex)

Men's European Championship

1957	*Rotterdam*	1st Hans Winkler on *Sonnenglanz*, W. Germany

		2nd Capt. B. de Fombelle on *Bucephale*, France
		3rd S. Oppes on *Pagoro*, Italy
1958	*Aachen*	1st F. Thiedemann on *Meteor*, W. Germany
		2nd Capt. Piero d'Inzeo on *The Rock*, Italy
		3rd Hans Winkler on *Halla*, W. Germany
1959	*Paris*	1st Capt. Piero d'Inzeo on *Uruguay*, Italy
		2nd P. J. d'Oriola on *Virtuoso*, France
		3rd F. Thiedemann on *Godewind*, W. Germany
1960	*No competition*	
1961	*Aachen*	1st David Broome on *Sunsalve*, Gt Britain
		2nd Capt. Piero d'Inzeo on *Pioneer*, Italy
		3rd Hans Winkler on *Romanus*, W. Germany
1962	*London*	1st David Barker on *Mister Softee*, Gt Britain
		2nd Tied: Hans Winkler on *Romanus*, W. Germany
		Capt. Piero d'Inzeo on *The Rock*, Italy
1963	*Rome*	1st G. Mancinelli on *Rockette*, Italy
		2nd Alwin Schockemohle on *Freiherr*, W. Germany
		3rd Harvey Smith on *O'Malley*, Gt Britain
1964	*No competition*	
1965	*Aachen*	1st Hermann Schridde on *Dozent*, W. Germany
		2nd A. Queipo de Lano on *Infernal*, Spain
		3rd Alwin Schockemohle on *Exakt*, W. Germany
1966[1]	*Lucerne*	1st Nelson Pessoa on *Gran Geste*, Brazil
		2nd Frank Chapot on *San Lucas*, U.S.A.
		3rd H. Arrambide on *Chimbote*, Argentine
1967	*Rotterdam*	1st David Broome on *Mister Softee*, Gt Britain
		2nd Harvey Smith on *Harvester*, Gt Britain [W. Germany
		3rd Alwin Schockemohle on *Donald Rex*,

[1] This was the last year that non-Europeans were eligible to compete.

171

1968	*No competition*	
1969	*Hickstead*	1st David Broome on *Mister Softee*, Gt Britain
		2nd Alwin Schockemohle on *Donald Rex*, W. Germany
		3rd Hans Winkler on *Enigk*, W. Germany
1970	*No competition*	
1971	*Aachen*	1st Hartwig Steenken on *Simona*, W. Germany
		2nd Harvey Smith on *Evan Jones*, Gt Britain
		3rd Capt. P. Weier on *Wulf*, Switzerland
1972	*No competition*	
1973	*Hickstead*	1st Paddy McMahon on *Pennwood Forge Mill*, Gt Britain
		2nd Alwin Schockemohle on *The Robber*, W. Germany
		3rd Hubert Parot on *Tic*, France

(After 1973 only one title in this championship, open to either sex)

EUROPEAN CHAMPIONSHIPS – SHOW JUMPING

1974	*No competition*	
1975	*Munich*	1st Alwin Schockemohle on *Warwick*, W. Germany
		2nd Hartwig Steenken on *Erle*, W. Germany
		3rd Sönke Sonksen on *Kwept*, W. Germany

EUROPEAN CHAMPIONSHIPS – THREE-DAY EVENT

1953	*Badminton*		
	Team	1st Gt Britain (J. R. Hindley on *Speculation*, Lt-Col. Frank Weldon on *Kilbarry*, A. E. Hill on *Bambi*)
		(No other team finished.)
	Individual	Major Lawrence Rook on *Starlight*, Gt Britain
1954	*Basle*	
	Team	1st Gt Britain (Lt-Col. Frank Weldon on *Kilbarry*, A. E. Hill on *Crispin*, Major L. Rook on *Starlight*, Miss Diana Mason on *Tramella*)
		2nd W. Germany
		(Only two teams finished.)

	Individual	A. E. Hill on *Crispin*, Gt Britain
1955	*Windsor*	
	Team	1st Gt Britain (Lt-Col. Frank Weldon on *Kilbarry*, A. E. Hill on *Countryman III*, Major L. Rook on *Starlight*, Miss Diana Mason on *Tramella*) 2nd Switzerland (Only two teams finished.)
	Individual	Lt-Col. Frank Weldon on *Kilbarry*, Gt Britain
1956	*No competition*	
1957	*Copenhagen*	
	Team	1st Gt Britain (Major Derek Allhusen on *Laurien*, Miss Sheila Willcox on *High and Mighty*, E. Marsh on *Wild Venture*, Miss Diana Mason on *Tramella*) 2nd W. Germany 3rd Sweden
	Individual	Miss Sheila Willcox on *High and Mighty*, Gt Britain
1958	*No Competition*	
1959	*Harewood*	
	Team	1st W. Germany (August Lutke-Westhues on *Franko II*, Ottokar Pohlmann on *Polarfuchs*, S. Dehning on *Fechtlanze*, Reine Klimke on *Fortunat*) 2nd Gt Britain 3rd France
	Individual	Major H. Schwarzenbach on *Burn Trout*, Switzerland
1960	*No competition*	
1961	*No competition*	
1962	*Burghley*	
	Team	1st Russia (L. Baklyshkin on *Khirurg*, G. Gaziumov on *Granj*, P. Deev on *Satrap*, S. Mursalimov on *Sekret*) 2nd Ireland 3rd Gt Britain
	Individual	Capt. J. Templer on *M'Lord Connolly*, Gt Britain
1963	*No competition*	
1964	*No competition*	
1965	*Moscow*	
	Team	1st Russia (G. Gaziumov on *Granj*, S. Mursalimov on *Dzhigit*, Lev Baklyshkin on *Eulon*, A. Evdokimov on *Podarok*) 2nd Ireland 3rd Gt Britain
	Individual	M. Babiericki on *Volt*, Poland

1966   Epidemic of equine infectious anaemia stopped all European Events.

1967   *Punchestown*
       Team   1st Gt Britain (Martin Whiteley on *The Poacher*, Sgt Ben Jones on *Foxdor*, Major Derek Allhusen on *Lochinvar*, Richard Meade on *Barberry*)
                 2nd Ireland
                 3rd France
       Individual   Major Eddie Boylan on *Durlas Eile*, Ireland

1968   *No competition*
1969   *Haras du Pin*
       Team   1st Gt Britain (Major Derek Allhusen on *Lochinvar*, Richard Walker on *Pasha*, Sgt Ben Jones on *The Poacher*, Miss Hely Hutchinson on *Count Jasper*)
                 2nd Russia
                 3rd W. Germany
       Individual   Miss Mary Gordon-Watson on *Cornishman V*, Gt Britain

1970   *No competition*
1971   *Burghley*
       Team   1st Gt Britain (Richard Meade on *The Poacher*, Lt Mark Phillips on *Great Ovation*, Miss Mary Gordon-Watson on *Cornishman V*, Miss Debbie West on *Baccarat*)
                 2nd Russia
                 3rd Ireland
       Individual   H.R.H. Princess Anne on *Doublet*, Gt Britain

1972   *No competition*
1973   *Kiev*
       Team   1st W. Germany (H. Blocker on *Albrant*, H. Karsten on *Sioux*, K. Mergler on *Vaibel*, H. Klugman on *El Paso*)
                 2nd Russia
                 3rd Gt Britain
       Individual   A. Evdokimov on *Jeger*, Russia

1974   *No competition*
1975   *Luhmühlen*
       Team   1st Russia (Vladimir Tischkin on *Flot*, Vladimir Lanügin on *Refleks*, Viktor Kalinin on *Araks*, Peter Gornuschkoon on *Gusar*)
                 2nd Gt Britain
                 3rd W. Germany
       Individual   Miss Lucinda Prior-Palmer on *Be Fair*, Gt Britain

Harewood Horse Trials (Three-Day Event)

1953	Miss V. Machin-Goodall on *Neptune*, Gt Britain
1954	Miss P. Molteno on *Carmena*, Gt Britain
1955	Lt-Col. Frank Weldon on *Kilbarry*, Gt Britain
1956	Miss Sheila Willcox on *High and Mighty*, Gt Britain
1957	Ian Hume-Dudgeon on *Charleville*, Ireland
1958	O. Pohlmann on *Polarfuchs*, W. Germany
1959	European Championships
1960	No competition
	(For subsequent results *see* Burghley Horse Trials)

Junior Championship of Great Britain (Hickstead)

1969	John Evans on *Bambi*
1970	Miss Amanda Bakewell on *Star Flight*
1971	Miss D. Johnsey on *Champ IV*
1972	Christopher Farnsworth on *Last Reply*
1973	Miss Jane Smith on *Mystery XXX*
1974	Miss J. Germany on *Fate's Reward*
1975	Greg Gill on *Paper Clip*
1976	
1977	
1978	
1979	

King George V Gold Cup

1911	Capt. D. d'Exe on *Piccollo*, U.S.S.R.
1912	Lt Delvoie on *Murat*, Belgium
1913	Lt Baron de Meslon on *Amazone*, France
1914	Lt Baron de Meslon on *Amazone*, France
1915–19	No show
1920	Capt. de Laissardière on *Dignité*, France
1921	Lt-Col. G. Brooke on *Combined Training*, Gt Britain
1922	Major Count Antonelli on *Bluff*, Italy
1923	Capt. de Laissardière on *Grey Fox*, France
1924	Capt. Count Borsarelli on *Don Chisciotte*, Italy
1925	Lt-Col. M. Graham on *Bronco*, Gt Britain
1926	Lt F. H. Bontecou on *Ballymacshane*, U.S.A.
1927	Lt X. Bizard on *Quinine*, France
1928	Lt A. G. Martyr on *Forty Six*, Gt Britain
1929	Lt Gibault on *Mandarin*, France
1930	Lt J. A. Talbot-Ponsonby on *Chelsea*, Gt Britain
1931	Capt. J. Misonne on *The Parson*, Belgium
1932	Lt J. A. Talbot-Ponsonby on *Chelsea*, Gt Britain
1933	No show
1934	Lt J. A. Talbot-Ponsonby on *Best Girl*, Gt Britain

1935	Capt. J. J. Lewis on *Tramore Bay*, Ireland
1936	Cmdt J. G. O'Dwyer on *Limerick Lace*, Ireland
1937	Capt. X. Bizard on *Honduras*, France
1938	Major J. C. Friedberger on *Derek*, Gt Britain
1939	Lt A. Bettoni on *Adigrat*, Italy
1940–46	No show
1947	P. J. d'Oriola on *Marquis III*, France
1948	Lt-Col. H. M. Llewellyn on *Foxhunter*, Gt Britain
1949	Brian Butler on *Tankard*, Gt Britain
1950	Lt-Col. H. M. Llewellyn on *Foxhunter*, Gt Britain
1951	Capt. K. Barry on *Ballymeety*, Ireland
1952	Don Carlos Figueroa on *Gracieux*, Spain
1953	Lt-Col. H. M. Llewellyn on *Foxhunter*, Gt Britain
1954	F. Thiedemann on *Meteor*, W. Germany
1955	Lt-Col. Cartasegna on *Brando*, Italy
1956	W. Steinkraus on *First Boy*, U.S.A.
1957	Capt. P. d'Inzeo on *Uruguay*, Italy
1958	Hugh Wiley on *Master William*, U.S.A.
1959	Hugh Wiley on *Nautical*, U.S.A.
1960	David Broome on *Sunsalve*, Gt Britain
1961	Capt. P. d'Inzeo on *The Rock*, Italy
1962	Capt. P. d'Inzeo on *The Rock*, Italy
1963	Tommy Wade on *Dundrum*, Ireland
1964	W. Steinkraus on *Sinjon*, U.S.A.
1965	Hans Winkler on *Fortun*, W. Germany
1966	David Broome on *Mister Softee*, Gt Britain
1967	Peter Robeson on *Firecrest*, Gt Britain
1968	Hans Winkler on *Enigk*, W. Germany
1969	Ted Edgar on *Uncle Max*, Gt Britain
1970	Harvey Smith on *Mattie Brown*, Gt Britain
1971	Gerd Wiltfang on *Askan*, W. Germany
1972	David Broome on *Sportsman*, Gt Britain
1973	Paddy McMahon on *Pennwood Forge Mill*, Gt Britain
1974	Frank Chapot on *Mainspring*, U.S.A.
1975	Alwin Schockemohle on *Rex the Robber*, W. Germany
1976	
1977	
1978	
1979	

Leading Show Jumper of the Year

1949	Miss Pat Smythe on *Finality*
1950	Seamus Hayes on *Sheila*
1951	A. L. Beard on *Eforegiot*
1952	R. W. Hanson on *Snowstorm*
1953	Alan Oliver on *Red Admiral*
1954	Miss D. Palethorpe on *Earlsrath Rambler*

1955	Ted Williams on *Sunday Morning*
1956	Ted Williams on *Dumbell*
1957	Ted Williams on *Pegasus XIII*
1958	Tied: Ted Edgar on *Jane Summers*
	Miss Pat Smythe on *Mr Pollard*
1959	Harvey Smith on *Farmer's Boy*
1960	Ted Williams on *Pegasus XIII*
1961	Tied: D. B. Barker on *Lucky Sam*
	Miss C. Beard on *Mayfly*
1962	Miss Pat Smythe on *Flanagan*
1963	A. Fielder on *Vibart*
1964	Mrs C. D. Barker on *Atalanta*
1965	Harvey Smith on *Warpaint*
1966	A. Fielder on *Vibart*
1967	Harvey Smith on *Harvester VI*
1968	A. Fielder on *Vibart*
1969	Ted Edgar on *Uncle Max*
1970	Mrs Marion Mould (née Coakes) on *Stroller*
1971	Alan Oliver on *Pitz Palu*
1972	Miss Ann Moore on *Psalm*
1973	David Broome on *Sportsman*
1974	Graham Fletcher on *Tauna Dora*
1975	David Broome on *Sportsman*
1976	
1977	
1978	
1979	

OLYMPIC GAMES

1912 Stockholm

Show Jumping (9 nations)

Team	Gold Medal	Sweden (Count C. Lewenhaupt on *Medusa*, Count H. von Rosen on *Lord Iron*, F. Rosencrantz on *Drabant*, G. Kilman on *Gatan*)
	Silver Medal	France (Lt d'Astafort on *Amazone*, Lt Seigneur on *Cocotte*, F. Meyer on *Allons*, Capt. J. Cariou on *Mignon*)
	Bronze Medal	Germany (Prins Karl von Preussen on *Gibson Boy*, Count von Hohenau on *Pretty Girl*, Lt Deloch on *Hubertus*, S. Freyer on *Ultimus*)
Individual	Gold Medal	Capt. J. Cariou on *Mignon*, France
	Silver Medal	Lt von Krocker on *Dohna*, Germany
	Bronze Medal	Baron von Blommaert de Soye on *Clonmore*, Belgium

177

Three-Day Event (7 nations)

Team	Gold Medal	Sweden (Nils Aldercreutz on *Atout*, Lt Axel Nordlander on *Lady Artist*, Count Horn of Ammine on *Omen*, E. Casparsson on *Irmelin*)
	Silver Medal	Germany (Lt von Rochow on *Idealist*, Lt Lutcken on *Blue Boy*, Count von Schaesberg-Thannheim on *Grundsee*, Lt von Moers on *May Queen*)
	Bronze Medal	U.S.A. (John Montgomery on *Deceive II*, Guy Henry on *Chiswell*, Benjamin Lear on *Poppy*, Ephraim Graham on *Connie*)
Individual	Gold Medal	Lt Axel Nordlander on *Lady Artist*, Sweden
	Silver Medal	Lt von Rochow on *Idealist*, Germany
	Bronze Medal	Capt. J. Cariou on *Cocotte*, France

1916   Not held

1920   Antwerp

Show Jumping (6 nations)

Team	Gold Medal	Sweden (Count H. von Rosen on *Poor Boy*, D. Norling on *Eros*, C. Konig on *Tresor*)
	Silver Medal	Belgium (Count d'Oultremone on *Lord Kitchener*, Baron de Gaiffier on *Miss*, Lt Coumans on *Lisette*)
	Bronze Medal	Italy (S. de Rossi on *Neruccio*, Major A. Valerio on *Cento*, Lt T. Lequio on *Trebecco*)
Individual	Gold Medal	Lt T. Lequio on *Trebecco*, Italy
	Silver Medal	Major A. Valerio on *Cento*, Italy
	Bronze Medal	Capt. A. Lewenhaupt on *Mon Coeur*, Sweden

Three-Day Event (8 nations)

Team	Gold Medal	Sweden (Count Helmer Morner on *Germania*, Lt Age Lundstrom on *Yrsa*, George von Braum on *Diana*)
	Silver Medal	Italy (Giulio Cacciandra on *Faceto*, Garibaldi Spighi on *Othello*, Major Ettore Caffaratti on *Traditore*)
	Bronze Medal	Belgium (Roger M. d'Emans on *Sweet Girl*, Lt Lints on *Martha*, J. Bonvalet on *Wippelgem*)
Individual	Gold Medal	Count Helmer Morner on *Germania*, Sweden
	Silver Medal	Lt Age Lundstrom on *Yrsa*, Sweden
	Bronze Medal	Major Ettore Caffaratti on *Traditore*, Italy

1924 Paris

Show Jumping (*11 nations*)

Team	Gold Medal	Sweden (A. Thelming on *Loke*, A. Stahle on *Cecil*, Lt A. Lindstrom on *Anvers*)
	Silver Medal	Switzerland (H. Buhler on *Boy*, W. Stuber on *Girandole*, Lt A. Gemuseus on *Lucette*)
	Bronze Medal	Portugal (B. d'Almeida on *Reginald*, M. de Souza on *Avro*, M. d'Albuquerque on *Hetrago*)
Individual	Gold Medal	Lt A. Gemuseus on *Lucette*, Switzerland
	Silver Medal	Lt T. Lequio on *Trebecco*, Italy
	Bronze Medal	Lt A. Krolikiewicz on *Picador*, Poland

Three-Day Event (*13 nations*)

Team	Gold Medal	Netherlands (Lt Adolph van der Voort van Zijp on *Silver Piece*, C. F. Pahud de Mortanges on *Johnnie Walker*, G. P. de Kruyff on *Addis*)
	Silver Medal	Sweden (G. von Konig on *Bojan*, L. Sylvan on *Anita*, O. W. Hagelin on *Varius*)
	Bronze Medal	Italy (Emanuel di Pralorno on *Mount Felix*, Alessandro Alvisi on *Capiligo*, Alberto Lombardi on *Pimplo*)
Individual	Gold Medal	Lt Adolph van der Voort van Zijp on *Silver Piece*, Netherlands
	Silver Medal	Lt Frode Kirkeberg on *Metoo*, Denmark
	Bronze Medal	Major Sloan Doak on *Pathfinder*, U.S.A.

1928 Amsterdam

Show Jumping (*16 nations*)

Team	Gold Medal	Spain (Marquess de los Trujillos on *Zalamero*, J. N. Morenes on *Zapatoso*, J. G. Fernandez on *Revistado*)
	Silver Medal	Poland (K. Szosland on *Alli*, M. Antoniewicz on *Readglet*, G. Gzowski on *Mylord*)
	Bronze Medal	Sweden (K. Hansen on *Gerold*, C. Bjornstjerna on *Kornett*, E. Haltberg on *Loke*)

Individual Gold Medal   Capt. F. Ventura on *Eliot*, Czechoslovakia

Silver Medal   Capt. M. L. Bertran de Balanda on *Papillon*, France

Bronze Medal   Major C. Kuhn on *Pepita*, Switzerland

Three-Day Event (*17 nations*)

Team   Gold Medal   Netherlands (G. P. de Kruyff on *Va-t-En*, Adolph van der Voort van Zijp on *Silver Piece*, Lt C. Ferdinand Pahud de Mortanges on *Marcroix*)

Silver Medal   Norway (Arthur Qurst on *Hadalgo*, Eugen Johansen on *Baby*, Bjart Ording on *And-Over*)

Bronze Medal   Poland (J. Trenkwald on *Lwi Pazur*, Baron C. von Rommel on *Donzef*, M. Antoniewicz on *Moja Mila*)

Individual Gold Medal   Lt C. Ferdinand Pahud de Mortanges on *Marcroix*, Netherlands

Silver Medal   G. P. de Kruyff on *Va-t-En*, Netherlands

Bronze Medal   Major Bruno Neumann on *Ilja*, Germany

1932   Los Angeles

Show Jumping (4 nations)

No team award given as no team finished the course

Individual Gold Medal   Lt T. Nishi on *Uranus*, Japan

Silver Medal   Major H. Chamberlin on *Show Girl*, U.S.A.

Bronze Medal   Lt C. von Rosen on *Empire*, Sweden

Three-Day Event (5 nations)

Team   Gold Medal   U.S.A. (Lt Earl F. Thomson on *Jenny Camp*, Edwin Y. Argo on *Honolulu Tomboy*, Major H. Chamberlin on *Pleasant Smiles*)

Silver Medal   Netherlands (Lt C. Ferdinand Pahud de Mortanges on *Marcroix*, Karrel J. Schummelketel on *Duneltje*, Aernaut van Lennep on *Hank*)

No team Bronze Medal as only two teams finished

Individual Gold Medal   Lt C. Ferdinand Pahud de Mortanges on *Marcroix*, Netherlands

Silver Medal   Lt Earl F. Thomson on *Jenny Camp*, U.S.A.

Bronze Medal   Lt C. von Rosen on *Sunnyside Maid*, Sweden

1936 Berlin
Show Jumping (18 nations)

Team	Gold Medal	Germany (H. Brandt on *Alchimist*, M. von Barnekow on *Nordland*, Lt K. Hasse on *Tora*)
	Silver Medal	Netherlands (J. Greter on *Ernica*, H. van Schaik on *Santa Bell*, J. de Bruine on *Trixie*)
	Bronze Medal	Portugal (J. Beltrano on *Biscuit*, Marquess de Funchal on *Merle Blanc*, M. de Silva on *Fossette II*)
Individual	Gold Medal	Lt K. Hasse on *Tora*, Germany
	Silver Medal	Lt H. Rang on *Delphis*, Rumania
	Bronze Medal	Capt J. Platthy on *Selloe*, Hungary

Three-Day Event (19 nations)

Team	Gold Medal	Germany (Capt. Ludwig Stubbendorf on *Nurmi*, Rudolph Lippert on *Fasan*, Konrad Freiherr von Wagenheim on *Kurfurst*)
	Silver Medal	Poland (Henryk Rojcewicz on *Arlekin III*, Zdislaw Kawecki on *Bambino*, Severyn Kulesza on *Toska*)
	Bronze Medal	Gt Britain (Alec Scott on *Bob Clive*, Edward Howard-Vyse on *Blue Steel*, Richard Fanshawe on *Bowie Knife*)
Individual	Gold Medal	Capt. Ludwig Stubbendorf on *Nurmi*, Germany
	Silver Medal	Capt. Earl E. F. Thomson on *Jenny Camp*, U.S.A.
	Bronze Medal	Capt. Hans Lunding on *Jason*, Denmark

1940 and 1944 Not held

1948 London
Show Jumping (15 nations)

Team	Gold Medal	Mexico (Lt R. Uriza on *Hatuey*, Col. Cortes H. Mariles on *Arete*, A. Valdes on *Chihuahua*)
	Silver Medal	Spain (J. Garcia Cruz on *Bizarro*, J. N. Morenes on *Quorum*, G. J. Ponce de Leon on *Farajido*)
	Bronze Medal	Gt Britain (Lt-Col. Harry Llewellyn on *Foxhunter*, Major H. M. V. Nicholl on *Kilgeddin*, Major A. Carr on *Monty*)
Individual	Gold Medal	Col. Cortes H. Mariles on *Arete*, Mexico

Silver Medal Lt R. Uriza on *Hatuey*, Mexico
Bronze Medal Chev. J. F. M. d'Orgeix on *Sucre de Pomme*, France

Three-Day Event (16 nations)

Team Gold Medal U.S.A. (Lt-Col. Frank S. Henry on *Swing Low*, Charles Anderson on *Reno Palisade*, Capt. Earl F. Thomson on *Reno Rhythm*)

Silver Medal Sweden (Capt. J. R. Selfelt on *Claque*, Sigurd Svensson on *Dust*, Nils-O. Stahre on *Komet*)

Bronze Medal Mexico (Col. Cortes H. Mariles on *Parral*, Raul Campero on *Tatahumara*, Joaquin Solano on *Malinche*)

Individual Gold Medal Capt. Bernard Chevallier on *Aiglonne*, France

Silver Medal Lt-Col. Frank S. Henry on *Swing Low*, U.S.A.

Bronze Medal Capt. J. R. Selfelt on *Claque*, Sweden

1952 Helsinki

Show Jumping (20 nations)

Team Gold Medal Gt Britain (Lt-Col. Harry Llewellyn on *Foxhunter*, W. H. White on *Nizefela*, Lt-Col. D. N. Stewart on *Aherlow*)

Silver Medal Chile (R. Echeverria on *Lindo Pearl*, O. Cristi on *Bambi*, C. Mendoza on *Pillan*)

Bronze Medal U.S.A. (A. McCashin on *Miss Budweiser*, J. Russell on *Democrat*, William Steinkraus on *Hollandia*)

Individual Gold Medal P. J. d'Oriola on *Ali Baba*, France

Silver Medal O. Cristi on *Bambi*, Chile

Bronze Medal F. Thiedemann on *Meteor*, W. Germany

Three-Day Event (21 nations)

Team Gold Medal Sweden (Hans G. von Blixen-Finecke on *Jubal*, Nils-O. Stahre on *Komet*, Karl Frolen on *Fair*)

Silver Medal W. Germany (Dr Wilhelm Busing on *Hubertus*, Klaus Wagner on *Dachs*, Otto Rothe on *Trux von Kamax*)

Bronze Medal U.S.A. (Charles Hough Jnr on *Cassavellanus*, Walter Staley on *Graigwood Park*, John Wofford on *Benny Grimes*)

Individual Gold Medal Hans G. von Blixen-Finecke on *Jubal*, Sweden

Silver Medal Lt Guy Lefrant on *Verdun*, France

Bronze Medal Dr Wilhelm Busing on *Hubertus*, W. Germany

1956 Stockholm

Show Jumping (25 nations)

Team Gold Medal W. Germany (Hans Winkler on *Halla*, F. Thiedemann on *Meteor*, A. Lutke-Westhues on *Ala*)

Silver Medal Italy (Lt Raimondo d'Inzeo on *Merano*, Capt. Piero d'Inzeo on *Uruguay*, S. Oppes on *Pagoro*)

Bronze Medal Gt Britain (W. H. White on *Nizefela*, Miss Pat Smythe on *Flanagan*, Peter Robeson on *Scorchin*)

Individual Gold Medal Hans Winkler on *Halla*, W. Germany

Silver Medal Lt Raimondo d'Inzeo on *Merano*, Italy

Bronze Medal Capt. Piero d'Inzeo on *Uruguay*, Italy

Three-Day Event (19 nations)

Team Gold Medal Gt Britain (Lt-Col. Frank Weldon on *Kilbarry*, Major Lawrence Rook on *Wild Venture*, A. E. Hill on *Countryman III*)

Silver Medal W. Germany (August Lutke-Westhues on *Trux von Kamax*, Klaus Wagner on *Prinzess*, Otto Rothe on *Sissi*)

Bronze Medal Canada (John Rumble on *Cilroy*, James Elder on *Colleen*, Brian Herbinson on *Tara*)

Individual Gold Medal Petrus Kastenman on *Iluster*, Sweden

Silver Medal August Lutke-Westhues on *Trux von Kamax*, W. Germany

Bronze Medal Lt-Col. Frank Weldon on *Kilbarry*, Gt Britain

1960 Rome
Show Jumping (18 nations)

Team   Gold Medal   W. Germany (Alwin Schockemohle on *Ferdl*, Hans Winkler on *Halla*, F. Thiedemann on *Meteor*)

Silver Medal   U.S.A. (G. Morris on *Sinjon*, Frank Chapot on *Trail Guide*, William Steinkraus on *Ksar d'Esprit*)

Bronze Medal   Italy (A. Oppes on *The Scholar*, Capt. Raimondo d'Inzeo on *Merano*, Capt. Piero d'Inzeo on *The Rock*)

Individual Gold Medal   Capt. Raimondo d'Inzeo on *Posillipo*, Italy

Silver Medal   Capt. Piero d'Inzeo on *The Rock*, Italy

Bronze Medal   David Broome on *Sunsalve*, Gt Britain

Three-Day Event (19 nations)

Team   Gold Medal   Australia (Lawrence Morgan on *Salad Days*, Neale Lavis on *Mirrabooka*, William Roycroft on *Our Solo*)

Silver Medal   Switzerland (Hans Schwarzenbach on *Burn Trout*, Anton Buhler on *Gay Spark*, Rudolf Gunthardt on *Atbara*)

Bronze Medal   France (Jack le Goff on *Image*, Guy Lefrant on *Nicias*, Jean Le Roy on *Garden*)

Individual Gold Medal   Lawrence Morgan on *Salad Days*, Australia

Silver Medal   Neale Lavis on *Mirrabooka*, Australia

Bronze Medal   Anton Buhler on *Gay Spark*, Switzerland

1964 Tokyo
Show Jumping (17 nations)

Team   Gold Medal   W. Germany (H. Schridde on *Dozent*, Hans Winkler on *Fidelitas*, K. Jarasinski on *Torro*)

Silver Medal   France (P. J. d'Oriola on *Lutteur B.*, Miss Janou Lefebvre on *Kenavo B*, Capt. Guy Lefrant on *Monsieur de Littry*)

Bronze Medal   Italy (Capt. Piero d'Inzeo on *Sunbeam*, Capt. Raimondo d'Inzeo on *Posillipo*, G. Mancinelli on *Rockette*)

Individual Gold Medal   P. J. d'Oriola on *Lutteur*, France

184

Silver Medal Hermann Schridde on *Dozent*, W.
Germany
Bronze Medal Peter Robeson on *Firecrest*, Gt
Britain

Three-Day Event (12 nations)
Team   Gold Medal   Italy (Mauro Checcoli on *Surbean*,
Paoli Angioni on *King*, Guiseppe
Ravano on *Royal Love*)
Silver Medal U.S.A. (Michael Page on *Grass-
hopper*, Michael Plumb on *Bold
Minstrel*, Kevin Freeman on
Gallopade)
Bronze Medal W. Germany (Fritz Ligges on
Donkosak, Horst Karsten on
Condora, Lt Gerhard Schultz on
Balza X)
Individual Gold Medal   Mauro Checcoli on *Surbean*, Italy
Silver Medal Carlos Moratorio on *Chalan*,
Argentina
Bronze Medal Fritz Ligges on *Donkosak*, W.
Germany

1968 Mexico
Show Jumping (15 nations)
Team   Gold Medal   Canada (Tom Gayford on *Big Dee*,
J. Day on *Canadian Club*, J. Elder
on *The Immigrant*)
Silver Medal France (Marcel Rozier on *Quo
Vadis*, Miss Janou Lefebvre on
Rocket, P. J. d'Oriola on *Nagir*)
Bronze Medal W. Germany (Hermann Schridde
on *Dozent*, Alwin Schockemohle
on *Donald Rex*, Hans Winkler on
Enigk)
Individual Gold Medal   William Steinkraus on *Snowbound*,
U.S.A.
Silver Medal Miss Marion Coakes on *Stroller*,
Gt Britain
Bronze Medal David Broome on *Mister Softee*,
Gt Britain

Three-Day Event (12 nations)
Team   Gold Medal   Gt Britain (Major Derek Allhusen
on *Lochinvar*, Miss Jane Bullen on
Our Nobby, Richard Meade on
Cornishman V, Sgt Ben Jones on
The Poacher)
Silver Medal U.S.A. (James Wofford on *Kilkenny*,
Michael Page on *Foster*, Kevin
Freeman on *Chalan*, Michael
Plumb on *Plain Sailing*)

	Bronze Medal	Australia (James Scanlon on *The Furtive*, Brian Cobcroft on *Depeche*, Wayne Roycroft on *Zhivago*, Bill Roycroft on *Warrathoola*)
Individual	Gold Medal	Jean-Jacques Guyon on *Pitou*, France
	Silver Medal	Major Derek Allhusen on *Lochinvar*, Gt Britain
	Bronze Medal	Michael Page on *Foster*, U.S.A.

1972 Munich

Show Jumping (17 nations)

Team	Gold Medal	W. Germany (Fritz Ligges on *Robin*, Gerd Wiltfang on *Askan*, Hartwig Steenken on *Simona*, Hans Winkler on *Torphy*)
	Silver Medal	U.S.A. (N. Shapiro on *Sloopy*, Kathy Kusner on *Fleet Apple*, Frank Chapot on *White Lightning*, William Steinkraus on *Main Spring*)
	Bronze Medal	Italy (Vittorio Orlandi on *Fulmer Feather Duster*, G. Mancinelli on *Ambassador*, Capt. Raimondo d'Inzeo on *Fiorello*, Col. Piero d'Inzeo on *Easter Light*)
Individual	Gold Medal	G. Mancinelli on *Ambassador*, Italy
	Silver Medal	Miss Ann Moore on *Psalm*, Gt Britain
	Bronze Medal	N. Shapiro on *Sloopy*, U.S.A.

Three-Day Event (19 nations)

Team	Gold Medal	Gt Britain (Miss Mary Gordon-Watson on *Cornishman V*, Mrs Bridget Parker on *Cornish Gold*, Lt Mark Phillips on *Great Ovation*, Richard Meade on *Laurieston*)
	Silver Medal	U.S.A. (Kevin Freeman on *Good Mixture*, Bruce Davidson on *Plain Sailing*, Michael Plumb on *Free and Easy*, James Wofford on *Kilkenny*)
	Bronze Medal	W. Germany (Harry Klugmann on *Christopher Robert*, Kurt Schultz on *Pisco*, Ludwig Goessing on *Chicago*, Horst Karsten on *Sioux*)
Individual	Gold Medal	Richard Meade on *Laurieston*, Gt Britain
	Silver Medal	A. Argenton on *Woodland*, Italy
	Bronze Medal	J. Jonsson on *Sarajevo*, Sweden

Pan American Games
(North and South American continents and Canada)

1951   Buenos Aires
Show Jumping
Team   Chile
Individual   Capt. A. Larraguibel, Chile
Three-Day Event
Team   Argentina
Individual   Capt. Julio C. Sagasta, Argentina
1955   Mexico
Show Jumping
Team   Mexico
Individual   Lt R. Vinals, Mexico
Three-Day Event
Team   Mexico
Individual   Walter Staley Jr, U.S.A.
1959   Chicago
Show Jumping
Team   U.S.A.
Individual   No classification
Three-Day Event
Team   Canada
Individual   Michael Page, U.S.A.
1963   Sao Paolo
Show Jumping
Team   U.S.A.
Individual   Miss Mary Mairs, U.S.A.
Three-Day Event
Team   U.S.A.
Individual   Michael Page, U.S.A.
1967   Winnipeg
Show Jumping
Team   Brazil
Individual   Jimmy Day, Canada
Three-Day Event
Team   U.S.A.
Individual   Michael Plumb, U.S.A.
1971   Cali
Show Jumping
Team   Canada
Individual   Miss Elisa P. de las Heras, Mexico
Three-Day Event
Team   Canada
Individual   Manuel Mendevil, Mexico
1975

President's Cup

1965	1st Gt Britain	35 points
	2nd W. Germany	31 points
	3rd Italy	30 points
1966	1st U.S.A.	27 points
	2nd Spain	26 points
	3rd France	20 points
1967	1st Gt Britain	37 points
	2nd W. Germany	26 points
	3rd Italy	21 points
1968	1st U.S.A.	34 points
	2nd Gt Britain	26 points
	3rd Tied: Italy	
	W. Germany	25 points
1969	1st W. Germany	39 points
	2nd Gt Britain	35 points
	3rd Italy	29 points
1970	1st Gt Britain	27.5 points
	2nd W. Germany	25 points
	3rd Italy	15 points
1971	1st W. Germany	37 points
	2nd Gt Britain	33 points
	3rd Italy	26 points
1972	1st Gt Britain	33 points
	2nd W. Germany	32 points
	3rd Italy	20 points
1973	1st Gt Britain	34 points
	2nd W. Germany	33 points
	3rd Switzerland	21 points
1974	1st Gt Britain	37 points
	2nd W. Germany	33.5 points
	3rd France	26 points
1975	1st W. Germany	38 points
	2nd Gt Britain	35 points
	3rd Tied: Italy	
	Belgium	22 points

Prince of Wales Cup

1909	France	1952	Gt Britain
1910	Belgium	1953	Gt Britain
1911	Russia	1954	Gt Britain
1912	Russia	1955	Italy
1913	Russia	1956	Gt Britain
1914	Russia (won outright)	1957	Gt Britain
1915-19	No show	1958	U.S.A.
1920	Sweden	1959	U.S.A.
1921	Gt Britain	1960	U.S.A.

1922	Gt Britain	1961	Italy
1923	Italy	1962	W. Germany
1924	Gt Britain	1963	Gt Britain
1925–28	No show	1964	Gt Britain
1929	Gt Britain	1965	Italy
1930	Gt Britain	1966	No competition owing to equine flu epidemic
1931	France		
1932	France		
1933	No show	1967	Gt Britain
1934	France	1968	U.S.A.
1935	Gt Britain	1969	W. Germany
1936	France	1970	Gt Britain
1937	Irish Free State	1971	Gt Britain
1938	Gt Britain	1972	Gt Britain
1939	Gt Britain	1973	W. Germany
1940–46	No show	1974	Gt Britain
1947	France	1975	Gt Britain
1948	U.S.A.	1976	
1949	Gt Britain	1977	
1950	Gt Britain	1978	
1951	Gt Britain	1979	

Queen Elizabeth II Cup

1949	Miss Iris Kellett on *Rusty*, Ireland
1950	Miss J. Palethorpe on *Silver Cloud*, Gt Britain
1951	Miss Iris Kellett on *Rusty*, Ireland
1952	Mrs G. Rich on *Quicksilver III*, Gt Britain
1953	Miss M. Delfosse on *Fanny Rosa*, Gt Britain
1954	Miss J. Bonnard on *Charleston*, France
1955	Miss Dawn Palethorpe on *Earlsrath Rambler*, Gt Britain
1956	Miss Dawn Palethorpe on *Earlsrath Rambler*, Gt Britain
1957	Miss Elizabeth Anderson on *Sunsalve*, Gt Britain
1958	Miss Pat Smythe on *Mr Pollard*, Gt Britain
1959	Miss A. Clement on *Nico*, W. Germany
1960	Miss Sue Cohen on *Clare Castle*, Gt Britain
1961	Lady Sarah Fitzalan-Howard on *Oorskiet*, Gt Britain
1962	Mrs Judy Crago on *Spring Fever*, Gt Britain
1963	Miss Julie Nash on *Trigger Hill*, Gt Britain
1964	Miss Gillian Makin on *Jubilant*, Gt Britain
1965	Miss Marion Coakes on *Stroller*, Gt Britain
1966	Miss A. Roger Smith on *Havana Royal*, Gt Britain
1967	Miss B. Jennaway on *Grey Lag*, Gt Britain
1968	Mrs Frank Chapot on *White Lightning*, U.S.A.
1969	Mrs Alison Dawes (née Westwood) on *The Maverick VII*, Gt Britain
1970	Miss A. Drummond-Hay on *Merely-a-Monarch*, Gt Britain

1971	Mrs Marion Mould (née Coakes) on *Stroller*, Gt Britain
1972	Miss Ann Moore on *Psalm*, Gt Britain
1973	Tied: Miss Ann Moore on *Psalm*, Gt Britain Mrs Alison Dawes (née Westwood) on *Mr Banbury* (*The Maverick VII*), Gt Britain
1974	Mrs Jean Davenport on *All Trumps*, Gt Britain
1975	Mrs Jean Davenport on *Hang On*, Gt Britain
1976	
1977	*Liz Edgar on Everst wallaby.*
1978	
1979	

WORLD CHAMPIONSHIPS – SHOW JUMPING
Ladies World Championship

1965	*Hickstead*	1st Miss Marion Coakes on *Stroller*, Gt Britain
		2nd Miss Kathy Kusner on *Untouchable*, U.S.A.
		3rd Miss Alison Westwood on *The Maverick VII*, Gt Britain
1970	*Copenhagen*	1st Miss Janou Lefebvre on *Rocket*, France
		2nd Mrs Marion Mould (née Coakes) on *Stroller*, Gt Britain
		3rd Miss A. Drummond-Hay on *Merely-a-Monarch*, Gt Britain
1974	*La Baule*	1st Mrs Janou Tissot (née Lefebvre) on *Rocket*, France
		2nd Miss Michelle McEvoy on *Mister Muskie*, U.S.A.
		3rd Mrs Barbara Kerr on *Magnor*, Canada

(After 1974 only one title in this championship, open to either sex)

Men's World Championship

1953	*Paris*	1st F. Goyoaga on *Quorum*, Spain
		2nd F. Thiedemann on *Diamant*, W. Germany
		3rd P. J. d'Oriola on *Ali Baba*, France
1954	*Madrid*	1st Hans Winkler on *Halla*, W. Germany
		2nd P. J. d'Oriola on *Arlequin*, France
		3rd F. Goyoaga on *Quorum*, Spain
1955	*Aachen*	1st Hans Winkler on *Halla*, W. Germany

		2nd Lt Raimondo d'Inzeo on *Nadir*, Italy
		3rd R. Dallas on *Bones*, Gt Britain
1956	*Aachen*	1st Lt Raimondo d'Inzeo on *Merano*, Italy
		2nd F. Goyoaga on *Fahemkonig*, Spain
		3rd F. Thiedemann on *Meteor*, W. Germany
1960	*Venice*	1st Capt. Raimondo d'Inzeo on *Gowran Girl*, Italy
		2nd C. Delia on *Huipil*, Argentina
		3rd David Broome on *Sunsalve*, Gt Britain
1966	*Buenos Aires*	1st P. J. d'Oriola on *Pomone*, France
		2nd A. de Bohorques on *Quizas*, Spain
		3rd Capt. Raimondo d'Inzeo on *Bowjack*, Italy
1970	*La Baule*	1st David Broome on *Beethoven*, Gt Britain
		2nd G. Mancinelli on *Fidux*, Italy
		3rd Harvey Smith on *Mattie Brown*, Gt Britain
1974	*Hickstead*	1st Hartwig Steenken on *Simona*, W. Germany
		2nd Eddie Macken on *Pele*, Ireland
		3rd Hugo Simon on *Lavendel*, Austria

(After 1974 only one title in this championship, open to either sex)

1978 — 1st Gerd Wiltfang on Roman, W. Germany / 2nd Eddie Macken on Boomerang, Ireland / 3rd Mike Mac on Jet Run, U.S. [handwritten]

WORLD CHAMPIONSHIPS – THREE-DAY EVENT

1966	*Burghley*		
	Team	1st Ireland (Major Eddie Boylan on *Durlas Eile*, Miss P. Moreton on *Loughlin*, Miss V. Freeman-Jackson on *Sam Weller*, T. Brennan on *Kilkenny*)
		2nd Argentina
		(Only two teams finished)
	Individual	Capt. C. Moratorio on *Chalan*, Argentina
1970	*Punchestown*		
	Team	1st Gt Britain (Miss Mary Gordon-Watson on *Cornishman V*, Richard Meade on *The Poacher*, Lt Mark Phillips on *Chicago III*, Stewart Stevens on *Benson*)
		2nd France
		(Only two teams finished)

191

PLAN OF THE
NATIONS CUP COURSE
Prince of Wales Trophy
Hickstead
20 July 1975

DEVIL'S
DYKE

OXER **6**

1

TV &
JUDGES

START

'THE FUNNEL'

12c

12b

12

13

7 WA

FINISH

STAND

CLUB
HOUSE